MW00636377

KAFFE FASSETT'S TIMELESS THEMES

KAFFE FASSETT'S TIMELESS THEMES

23 New Quilts
Inspired by Classic Patterns

KAFFE FASSETT WITH LIZA PRIOR LUCY

PHOTOGRAPHS BY DEBBIE PATTERSON
ADDITIONAL PHOTOGRAPHY BY BRANDON MABLY

Abrams, New York

TO BRANDON MABLY,

for his consistent, inspired support

CONTENTS

INTRODUCTION

I WAS FASCINATED to learn recently that anthropologists have discovered that Neanderthal humans were interested in pattern and decoration. So, it's one of the most basic instincts of a human to create a pleasing order with the objects and parameters of their environment.

As a young boy, nothing intrigued me more than arranging pebbles, seashells, or sandcastles on a beach. Flower petals and leaves in a garden tickled my pattern-making brain. My mother, operating on a budget, went to builders' yards to source mill ends (wood scraps) that we (as toddlers) could use as building blocks. My brother and I kept out of her hair for hours while we built palaces with the ends of two-by-fours and dowels, etc., from those wood workers.

My earliest memories of pattern were of pretty stones in jewelry and the dress fabrics Mother and her friends would wear. When I was able to peruse books on my own, I zapped right into ethnic cultures—Native American Indian blankets, bowls, baskets, and kachina dolls that used old patterns constructed by people in the Hopi community, with their faces painted with patterns, spelled an alluring world to me. African cultures that painted their faces, braided their hair, and wore strongly patterned clothes filled my young imagination with a longing to find a more exotic world than the conforming American one I observed outside my family. For my family was definitely bohemian. Colorful paintings and furnishings filled our houses, and the friends my mother cultivated were rugged individualists.

Recognizing that I showed a fascination with anything creative, my mother made a point of getting me to any dance or colorful theatre that came to our nearest town of Carmel, California. We lived thirty miles (forty-eight km) outside of Carmel in a very wild but colorful community on the coast called Big Sur. Living there, my mind was filled with dynamic images from films like *The Red Shoes* and *Henry V*, and from exotic theatre like Kabuki or Balinese dance.

Brandon and Kaffe hanging the Suzani quilt on the gates of Smithfield Market in London

As I got older, I continued to study pattern and design all around me. The thing that amazes me is that it took so long for my obsession with pattern and color to find its perfect outlet in designing prints for patchwork. I love the world of patchwork quilts—geometric layouts created out of patterned cloth that light up the corners of our rooms and add a daily joy to our senses.

I started my life in patchwork with a collection of colorful striped fabrics that were handwoven in India. The opportunity to work with weavers in India was a priceless experience, primarily because ethnic textiles have always intrigued me. To explore cultures that have traditions of embroidery, carpet making, and decorative weaving was exciting and exotic because I grew up in a country that didn't seem to have any textile traditions. Actually, I was to discover later that America makes up for that in its rich history of quilting.

When the woven fabrics from India turned out to inspire enthusiasm among quilters, I was asked to design print fabrics to go along with the woven stripes. Remembering the quilts I'd seen and loved in English country houses, I was captivated by the idea of large-scale florals and paisleys. My first print collections included large Swiss chard plants, overblown roses, cabbages, and big geometric patterns. At first,

Tori gates at the Fushimi Shrine, Kyoto, Japan

these large-scale prints, with deep, rich colors, seemed to terrify the retail shops that were more accustomed to small-scale, traditional prints in tasteful palettes.

My patchwork designs are also influenced by my travels and interest in other cultures. I recognized right away that Japan had a culture with a refined delight in pattern and color. Its richly decorated kimonos and the sets of the great Kabuki theatre really haunted my charged, over-stimulated mind. When I finally got to Japan, decades later, I was thrilled to find it really was a culture that adored and played with patterns on a grand scale. My most potent memory was of a steep path of massive orange *torii* gates winding up the mountain at the Fushimi Inari Shrine in Kyoto. The gates were donated to the shrine, and because many were quite old, they were weathered to different shades of orange and red. Each gate was about 3 to 6 feet (1 to 3 meters) apart. These rich tones created a warm tunnel snaking up the hillside for miles. It was the most extreme, scaled-up work of pattern I had ever experienced.

Since then, I've traveled to many places that embrace pattern as extreme decoration, such as the Ndebele community in South Africa, where they paint the walls of their houses in bold geometric patterns with startling colors. One of my strongest ethnic influences is the textile called *suzani,* from Central Asia. Suzani is the name

Ndebele painted village in South Africa

of a large group of embroideries from Tajikistan, Uzbekistan, Kazakhstan, and other countries. Because it is a tradition handed down for generations, many inventive variations on the theme of circular (mostly red) motifs have evolved. I have created many suzani-inspired designs in needlepoint and printed fabrics, and I have also based one of my quilt patterns on an antique suzani. The most popular idea based on these joyous circular motifs is a knit design I devised in the late seventies called Persian Poppy. This pattern involved tying several colored yarns together and knitting a multicolored series of round shapes, which meant every version of this knit was unique. The knitter never knew which color would appear next in the changing sequence of colors. My design partner, Brandon Mably, has traveled the world teaching workshops on the Persian Poppy, which remains a favorite of many knitters.

The end result of one of Brandon's knit classes—twenty-five versions of my Persian Poppy design

Of course I was drawn to the infinite variety of tiles created in this world. Holland, with its charming blue and white tiles up staircases and surrounding every fireplace, delighted me. Spain was a revelation. Entire walls of brilliantly colored tiles in restaurants, a bridge covered in patterned tiles, and parks with murals in tiles made more bursts of happiness for me. All of these are examples of the great variety of styles the world has to offer a budding designer.

Before the 1980s, I was only interested in pattern as it appeared on the objects in my still life paintings, as I was trying to be a serious "fine" artist. Looking back, it's interesting to see that I used quilts in many of my still lifes whenever I could find a good one. I often scoured charity shops or borrowed old quilts from friends to create fascinating texture and color. I soon realized those old quilts had as much intrigue as any painting I'd come across.

About the same time, when I discovered a stash of subtly colored yarns in a Scottish mill and couldn't resist combining them in knitted garments, all my pent-up fascination with pattern came tumbling out as I searched for motifs to knit. After producing a successful book on knitting, *Glorious Knits*, I turned to needlepoint as a way of playing with more figurative subjects in wool. Those textiles were very interesting to me, but I felt it was time to get back to painting. I completed several mural commissions and had shows of my canvasses in New York. But when my friend Liza Prior Lucy tempted me to design patchwork, I was soon drawn into a world that has totally captivated me.

Liza was a yarn rep living in Pennsylvania and had been a champion of my first knitting book, helping others in the industry to see its value. At the time, she had been making quilts for her firstborn, and her growing enthusiasm made her feel that my eye for pattern and color would find a good home in the patchwork world. We met up and drove to every quilt shop in her area. In those days, Pennsylvania had a glut of shops selling traditional and contemporary patchwork fabrics. What an eye-opener that was for me to be exposed to all the color and pattern that was lurking in these amazing shops.

As I visited more and more American shops with Liza, I soon observed that the patterns on the prints were mostly medium- to small-scale. I longed for the large-scale roses and hollyhocks with trailing fat ribbons I'd seen on British quilts.

Just before I'd gone on this patchwork hunt with Liza, I'd been on a trip to India with Brandon. We'd been asked by the nonprofit Oxfam to offer creative support to a group of weavers working in a very remote region of India to produce fabric that would appeal to a Western market. I worked with the weavers to create samples of various scales and colors of stripes for the charity. When I noticed that these textiles were being marketed simply as duvet covers, I offered these colorful weaves to Westminster Fiber (now FreeSpirit Fabrics). Westminster had great success with those woven stripes in the quilt market, but they wanted a collection of prints to sell with the stripes, so I was asked to design some. My first thought was to create large-scale, so that first Swiss chard design was bold indeed. I also used an ancient chunk of Roman glass, studded with small circular motifs, as inspiration for my small-scale print. It says a lot that so many years later, this first print, called Roman Glass, is still in our Classics collection with a dozen or so colorways that remain popular among quilters.

Close-up of a mural in the United States

In the 1970s, the prestigious Whitney Museum of American Art in New York mounted a blockbuster show of quilts on their walls instead of their usual modern fare. The art market of the world sat up and took notice of this hidden gem in American culture. I too, as a budding artist, was astounded at the power and fascination of these works. All of my childhood and early traveler impressions started dancing in my mind as I painted out my first collections of prints for the patchwork market.

After I began to design more collections of quilt fabric, I realized that instead of trying to reinvent the wheel and come up with totally modern concepts, I was much more satisfied with reconstructing the great store of images I'd come across on my travels and visits to antique shops, and in the perusing of books on the world's decorative arts. This approach seemed to satisfy my readers as they recognized patterns and motifs from their past as well. It made me realize that the cultures that embraced pattern have developed a vocabulary of motifs that has gradually evolved over the years as each artisan has brought their own personality to a given theme.

Philip Jacobs creates beautifully rendered, large-scale florals, and figurative subjects such as feathers and shells that are inspired by his vast archive of vintage botanical paintings, wallpapers, and furnishing fabrics. Recognizing his talent, I asked him to join my team to create yearly collections. When Philip brings me his latest designs, I select six for that season and paint out colorways (different moods for each design). My partner, Brandon Mably, produces his own special line of witty and lively designs that have a graphic directness of form that contrasts well with Philip Jacobs's and my more detailed work.

So, that's what this book is all about: how three designers—Brandon Mably, Philip Jacobs, and I—have taken motifs from carpets, textiles, pottery, and wall decorations made by hardworking, instinctively creative people of the past. Together we are known as the Kaffe Fassett Collective. The fabrics we create evolve as we observe how quiltmakers across the globe create their own quilts from our annual collections of patterns and palettes. It's always a thrill for us to see how our prints are put to uses we never dreamed of.

The three artists in the Kaffe Fassett Collective are rarely photographed together! Here are (from left) Brandon Mably, Kaffe Fassett, and Philip Jacobs photographed in London in late 2021.

Color and scale seem to be the strongest elements that distinguish our collections. I go for high color, mostly because it always gives me a psychological lift whenever I see someone wearing strong color. I'm always inspired when I come across examples of high color in the decorative arts in museums and grand houses in our world travels. Brandon and I have been blessed with many invitations to teach, lecture, and exhibit our textiles in museums all over the world, and as a result we have many opportunities to steep ourselves in other cultures. We bring back books and artifacts to remind us of our travels, and we often incorporate vintage themes into our textile designs. I'm particularly interested in how a motif differs as a printed fabric, or a stitched needlepoint, or a knitted design. Often the things we collect are porcelain vases or bowls with lively decorations. Beaded bags and painted fans also figure as inspiration, so you'll see examples of these in the chapters in this book.

Making this book has given me the delightful task of rummaging in our fabric archives to find examples in themes in order to make quilts that demonstrate the different motifs that we return to over and over again in our design collections. I hope these ideas stimulate you to create quilts of different collections you come across in your never-ending hunt for expressive raw materials.

Because I've raided my fabric archives that go back years, many of the prints in quilts in this book are no longer available. I have included a few quilts with our most recent prints and our non-changing Classics range so that those who choose to follow recipes can do so. But this book should encourage you to delve into your stashes, your local shops, and, best of all, upcycled finds from local charity shops to create your own personal versions of these themed quilts. I can't wait to see what you come up with! Remember, our best-selling fabric is our neutral design wall, a flannel, gridded textile that holds your cut pieces of fabric, allowing you to stand back from a quilt layout and edit out weak areas.

My hope is that my creative readers will use this book as a gateway to explore their own objects and fabrics that reflect their personal choice of aesthetic. Doing so will allow each creative soul to add more juice and panache to their textiles, be they stitched, knitted, or gloriously patchworked together.

Kaffe and Brandon hanging the Sunrise quilt on a shopfront on Aberfeldy Street in London

ABERFELDY
big local
39

E ABERFELDY
Londis
CYCLES

Our Photo Locations

Once our quilts were all designed and being made up, Brandon and I started wracking our brains as to where to shoot them in sympathetic surroundings. We toyed with flying to America and other locations, but during our online search for colorful backgrounds, we came across the "most colorful street in London."

Aberfeldy Street is a small street of shops and businesses, a short walk from East India Dock Road in the Poplar area of London's East End. During lockdown, in the summer of 2020, Poplar HARCA (Housing and Regeneration Community Association) commissioned this public artwork in Aberfeldy Street, under the guidance of designers Jan Kattein Architects and Meanwhile Space. They used local residents' donations of old clothes and textiles as inspiration and created a wonderful collection of bright-colored patterns. Needless to say, it was an ideal atmosphere for our quilts.

This tiny street that sits among undistinguished London East End housing and cold, modern high-rise office buildings, has become a beacon of sunny joyfulness. Another rare example in a mostly monochrome world that bright color can lift and inspire humanity. I salute the community and painters of this magical street for their remarkable creativity.

Previous page and above: Aberfeldy Street's colorful renditions of local fabrics

Another location that also uses panels of strong pattern is Waithman Street, which is really a sidewalk running from Black Friars Lane to Pilgrim Street along the back wall of 100 New Bridge Street, near the city of London. My potter friend Rupert Spira was commissioned to create panels of his beautifully colored, handmade stoneware tiles for this building. Created in 1992, each panel is about eight feet (2.5 meters) tall and four feet (1.25 meters) across. Made of around 18,000 tiles glazed in reds, blues, turquoise, green, and gray, the murals form optical illusions and run the length of the rear elevation of the building. Because they are behind the building, with little traffic, few people ever see them, so we found ourselves in Waithman Street with a quiet place to hang and photograph our quilts.

Some of the tile panels made by Rupert Spira that made such colorful backdrops for our quilts

Chapter One

BOLD STRIPES

Knitted striped throw and needlepoint cushions by Kaffe

A BOLD STRIPE is probably one of the world's most basic and striking patterns. I think of extra-wide red and white striped buildings in India, awning stripes in blue and white over shop fronts and on deck chairs along the beach in England, and black and yellow stripes on signs and police tape everywhere that create a very effective warning. Another use of stripes that always gets my attention is circus tents—the high contrast of, say, scarlet and yellow stripes on circus tents is eye catching and signals FUN!

One of the most obvious things about stripes is the direction in which you place them in your quilt layout. All the same direction (vertical or horizontal) creates an interesting tension to my eye, whereas some vertical and some horizontal is livelier. I often get my students in workshops to place the few stripes they are adding to a scrappy quilt horizontally—that gives a calmer feel to the mix.

You will notice that in my Corrugated quilt in this chapter, I've kept all the stripes vertical, whereas in my Striped Squares quilt they are mixed. I've used mostly my handwoven stripes in these quilts, but think of the fun you could have plundering charity shops for all manner and scale of stripes on clothing, and then using these finds in a quilt. I don't make any effort to line up stripes; I just sew them as they fall and enjoy the randomness.

My first experience designing stripes was the multicolored handwoven ones in India. These beautiful woven, handkerchief-weight fabrics started my life as a patchwork textile designer. The first collection continued as part of our range for years, which is very rare in the patchwork world, where designs come and go at a fierce rate. Most designs, no matter how brilliantly successful, are replaced with a new collection within six months. These woven stripes lasted for several years in our collection, but as eye-catching as these multitoned stripes were, I started finding basic two-color stripes more useful in my patchworks. In fact, my latest collections of handwovens have two-toned stripes along with single-color shot cottons where the warp is one color and the weft another, so the fabric shimmers when seen from different angles.

A great inspiration for me are the Indian miniature paintings that are often chockablock with rich colored detail, burgeoning gardens or banquets in massively patterned interiors, and crowds of people in wonderful outfits. What always stands out to me amongst all the dancing color and pattern are the people who wear a black-and-white or blue-and-white striped coat. That crisp, high contrast is so fresh, especially in a complex-colored setting.

Another great ethnic inspiration is the Japanese *boro* panels. These are the work clothes of Japanese farmers from long ago who, being thrifty, constantly patched their clothes as their handsome, handwoven indigo outfits wore thin. Since they are mostly brown and deep blue colors, the results are close-toned arrangements of stripes and plaids overstitched with white cotton stab stitches. The results thrill me, and I was fired up to attempt my own variation on boro textiles in this book.

Previous spread left, clockwise from top left: Mosaic panel created by Brandon for Highland Stoneware Pottery in Ullapool, in the North West Highlands of Scotland; wood paneling in Hastings; hand-sewn quilt made by Kaffe and his sister Kim; beach huts at Hastings; wooden "Crazy Eights" quilt by Laura Petrovich-Cheney; Kaffe's Regimental Ties print in the Multi colorway; French coffee bowls from Kaffe's collection

Previous spread right: Kaffe's Serape Stripe print in the Bold colorway

BORO

I am so often knocked sideways by the inventive uses of printed fabrics in vintage quilt books, but in recent years I've come across equally inspiring finds in the world of woven textiles. Many of the antique cloth pieces used by Japanese farmers were made from hand-dyed indigo textiles. But some were also handwoven stripes, usually in black, browns, and indigo blues. This consistent palette magnifies the variations in the scale of stripes and plaids. Partly because they are so limited in color, the subtle differences create a stunning vibration that has me returning over and over to these intense patchwork panels.

I've taken my darkest woven stripes to place on an inky background in my homage to this form. I feel this is a quilt that would suit a nature that is moved by dark, subtle structure and balance. Of course, it could be done in any set of stripes, perhaps all neutrals. Or, dark-light striped fabrics could make a contrasting variation; or try it using the palette and stripes of the awning squares on page 22.

I've long admired the *kantha* pieces I've seen from India that usually patch recycled saris together and use long running stitches over the whole surface. Since the utility patchwork boro textiles do the same, I had a great time stitching over my raw edge patches with pale blue stitches. The Aurifil company has developed a great palette of colors that Liza Prior Lucy and I chose for our Glorious Kantha collection. I found this wonderful dark shopfront on Aberfeldy Street to place it on, and the effect delights me.

CORRUGATED

Raised in the countryside of the California coastline, I often came across old farm buildings with walls patched with rusty corrugated metal panels. By taking every darkish stripe I could find in my collections of prints and placing them in simple squares, I arrived at the impression I had of those rusty barn walls. I keep them all running in the same direction, you will notice. You could, of course, do this in any palette of colors you like. The delicate stripes of classic men's shirting fabrics would make a lovely soft quilt.

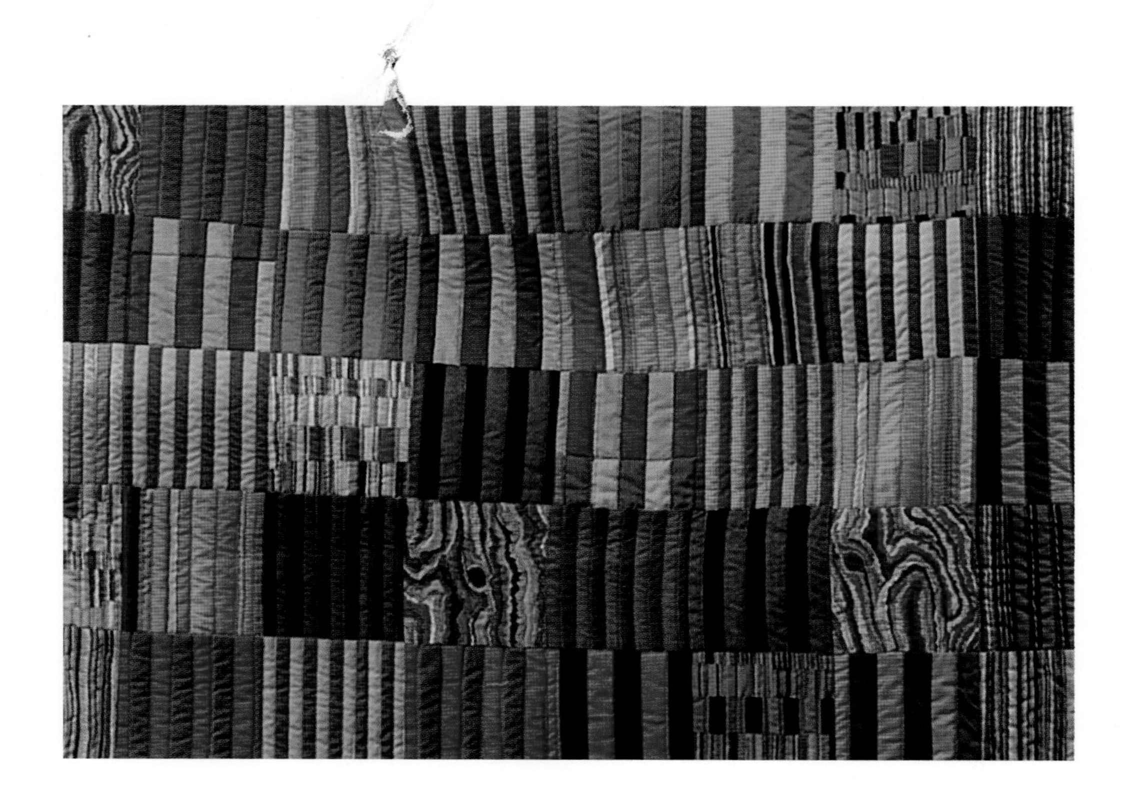

For this composition of stripes, I've used a medium-to-dark palette. There are a lot of stripes that go back to my early designing days, but my Indian shot stripes do most of all. The simple one-patch arrangement of squares helps you see all the variety of stripes within the quilt. There is something electric about all the stripes being vertical. Any collection of stripes could be used if you keep contrasts low. The stripes in the brick and the iron work here echo my quilt stripes.

STRIPED SQUARES

In my second hardcover book, *Passionate Patchwork*, I designed a quilt in classic men's shirt stripes that was a great favorite at the time. With fond memories of those many variations of stripes, cut into triangles to create multilayered boxes, I used the same layout with just two scales of stripes from my current collection. These handwoven stripes come in such delicious, dusty pastels and rich tones, they begged to be combined in a new version of a shirt-stripe quilt. To save time, I used the same placement of three different scales of stripes, just cut in squares and placed on my design wall. The effect was so pleasing that Liza told me, "I love it this way—don't cut them into triangles like the original version." So here it is, a simpler version. But I hope you feel, as I do, that it's full of life.

This bold use of stripes is softened by the dusty palette of my woven Indian stripes. I used one printed stripe of Brandon's in black and white to dot through the composition. I was delighted how it looked on these geometric tiles. This quilt could also be done in any collection of stripes you can find, light or dark.

Previous spread, clockwise from top left: Glazed jug in front of Missoni stripes card; hand-sewn quilt made by Kaffe and his sister Kim; Kaffe's Indian hand-woven Wide Stripe in the Burn colorway; Brandon's diagonal-stripe shirt; Kaffe's Indian hand-woven Wide Stripe in the Shell colorway; stack of striped mattresses in an Indian market; Kaffe's Chevron Stripe print in the Blue colorway; gorgeous patched robe on this figure in the Victoria and Albert Museum; Cloisonné cannister in a Paris window

Chapter Two

COMPLEX STRIPES

Left: Nautilus shell from Kaffe's collection; right: Textured and hand-painted wall in New Zealand

AFTER EXPLORING bold, regimented stripes, I turned my attention to the wonderfully organic stripes we see in natural settings—the tonal beauty of stripes on fungi, for instance. As a child I was thrilled to find mushrooms with flowing stripe designs growing on trees. Bird feathers provided an entirely new tonal, or sometimes highly colored, magical object. When I came to England in my late twenties, I found wonderful striped stones on the beaches, and I was thrilled to find whole mountainous cliffs of striated rock formations.

When I started traveling the world to teach and lecture, I discovered the Aboriginal paintings in Australia that have become a never-ending source of inspiration. These indigenous Australians paint in a mysteriously beautiful language of dots and stripes that has me mesmerized.

The zigzag is a great way to enliven a stripe. I started noticing these on Native American pottery and woven blankets. Missoni, the great Italian family of knitters, has used numerous versions of zigzags in their fashions and home furnishings for the past forty years.

One of the most striking stripe stories on this planet is the zebra. Their handsome bodies and angular faces are so amazingly defined by strong black and white stripes, and I'm always astounded at the artfulness of them when I see zebras in film. Another magical striped world is that of the natural formations of geodes and stones such as malachite and some marble. Here, color is so surprisingly rich and unexpected. To think that all those crystalline formations and fabulous colors are forming in the earth under our feet! Some of those very formations inspired Philip Jacobs to add wonderful, complex, organic stripes to our Kaffe Fassett Collective collections based on studies of geodes, feathers, and fungi.

The classic antique flame stitch led to one of my first stripe variations and falls in wonderfully with more organic, natural stripes. But of course, one of my favorite types of complex stripes is the zigzag. Brandon has created many lively renditions of zigzags that have entered our Classics range and often combine beautifully with our prints of florals and geometrics.

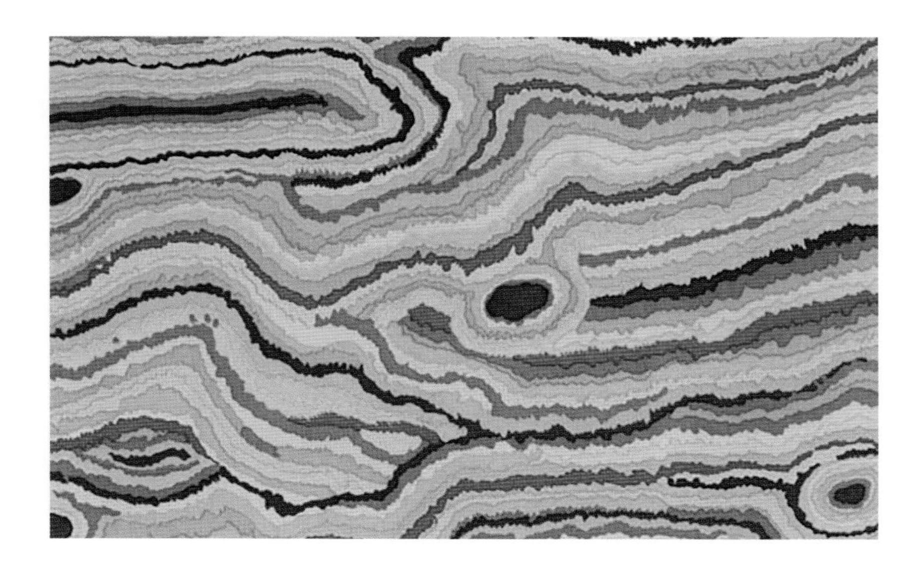

Kaffe's Jupiter print in the Purple colorway

Previous spread left, clockwise from top left: Kaffe's Beach Balls print in the Neutral colorway; Kaffe's Striped Herald print in the Contrast colorway; hand-knitted stripe design by Brandon; Kaffe's Paper Fans print in the Contrast colorway; Blue and white hand-knitted shawl by Kaffe; Kaffe's Flame Stitch print in the Pastel colorway; Brandon's Sharks Teeth print in the Blue colorway; glazed jug from a flea market, from Kaffe's collection

Previous spread right: Brandon's Zig Zag print in the Sky colorway

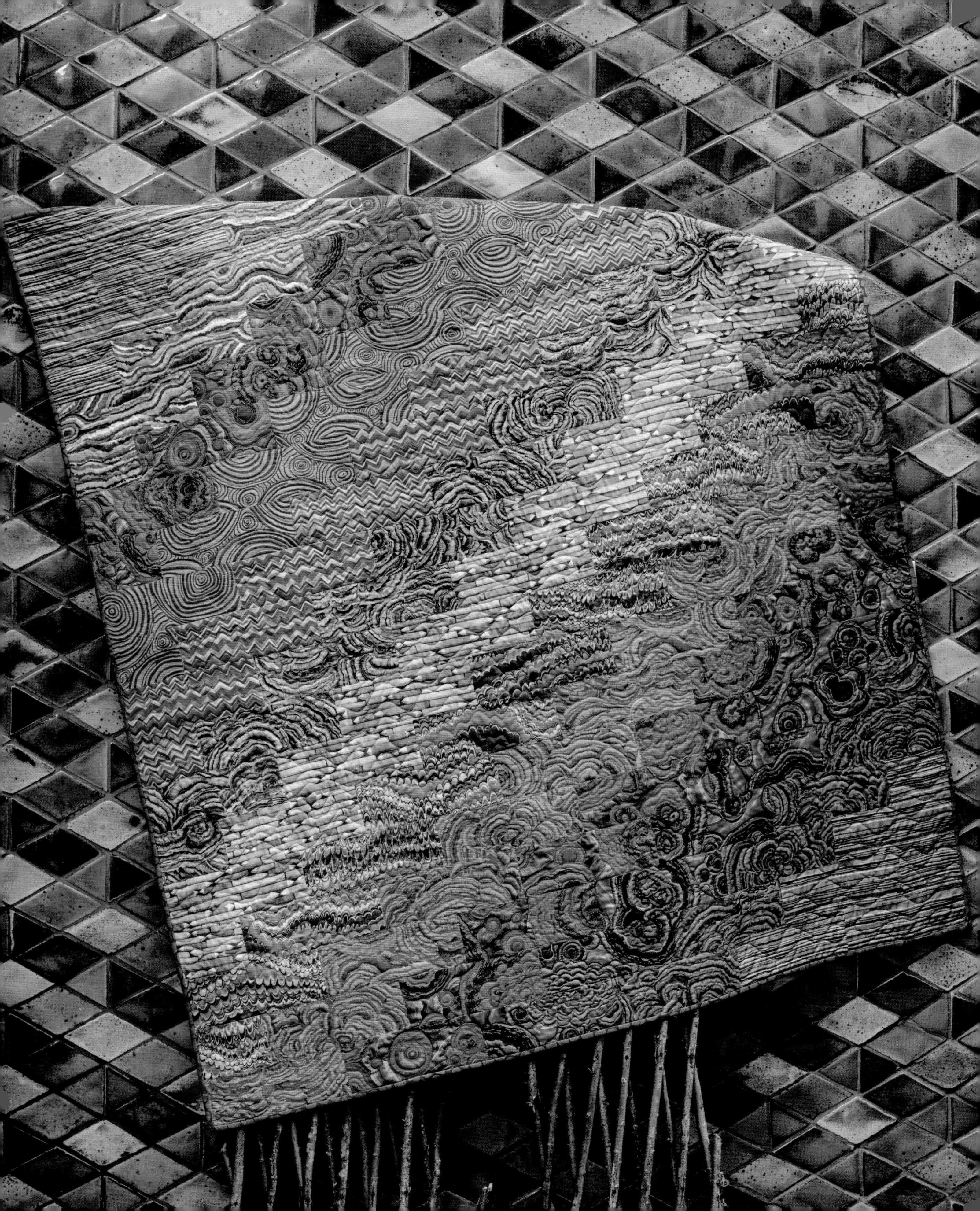

DIAGONAL BRICKS

I'm often moved by variations I see in rocky cliffs or marble panels that reveal the amazing movement of organic stone. There is something exciting about containing wild, meandering motifs inside set, rectangular shapes. In this quilt, I've taken another simple repeat-shape quilt with the same size bricks and staggered them diagonally. I've used all the prints I could find in my collections of organic stripes that flowed together. Rows of autumnal-colored Pencils fabric work well within the complexity of striped motifs and add a bit of wit to the arrangement. The combo of Brandon's Zig Zag with Philip's Agate and Tree Fungi forms and my marbled End Papers works a treat here too. Once these seemingly disparate bricks are stitched together, the rich palette creates a landscape-like impression. You could try this with any differing collection of stripes in any palette that suits you.

The rich tile colors contrast perfectly with the warm autumn palette of this quilt. As you can see, I like a bold print on the backs of my quilts. This backing is Jupiter in Brown.

OPTICAL STRIPES

This quilt plays with the concept of a neutral bed of texture with soft colored prints in various stripe forms rising up and glowing in the neutral space. The sashing is Brandon's Sharks Teeth. This jaunty black-and-white print has a lovely rhythm to it. It was fun digging into my historic fabric archive to find so many prints that relate to the wonky stripe story, and I'm sure you will have a creative time searching out all the stripe variations in your own stash, or in local shops. The key here is keeping a specific level of color, such as all dark, medium, or light tones in your prints, as this will help them hang together.

I like the way the pastel palette of my chosen prints almost disappears in frames in Brandon's Sharks Teeth and sashing in his Zig Zag in White. You could work this concept with a high-contrast sashing that frames your prints, instead of merging with them.

Previous spread, clockwise from top left: Hand-painted wall decoration in New Zealand; wire-covered bottle from South Africa; hand-knitted design for Peruvian Connection by Kaffe; Brandon's Zig Zag print in the Contrast colorway; beaded zigzag bracelet from South Africa; vintage Loan Star quilt from Kaffe's collection; natural stone beads; the wonderful natural stripes of a zebra; St. Mark's Cathedral in Venice; Kaffe's Paper Fans print in the Contrast colorway; Century Plant painting by Kaffe, 2008

Chapter Three

CIRCLES

Top: Venetian glass paperweights from Kaffe's collection; bottom: Kaffe's Millefiore print in the Aqua colorway

SO MANY THINGS in our lives rely on a circular form that any designer would be hard put not to employ them in their work. The very way we see is out of round eye lenses. So many fruits and flowers are so perfectly round that I could have easily done this whole book on the circular form. Intriguing circles can be found not just in nature, but also in the great human architecture of the past that produced round windows and domed doorways.

When I was growing up in California, my parents had a terrace laid at Nepenthe (our family restaurant, which sits on the cliff overlooking the Pacific Ocean) of redwood log slices that were organically round. Another memory from my California beginning is nasturtium plants that grew so lushly in many gardens. Their circular, bright green leaves balancing on slender stems always delighted me. Geranium leaves with colorful markings also caught my eye.

Beads and buttons, so often perfect circles, also became subjects for my fabric prints. I resisted doing the most classic of all circles, the basic polka dot, as I felt so many other fabric designers had done that motif forever. I suppose because I used unusual colorings when I did my first collection of spots, they caught on and became one of our most popular lines. We keep a large selection of them in our Classics range so quilters can use them year on year.

My very first fabric design was Roman Glass, and that study of ancient circles has been in our Classics range ever since. I added two designs based on artful glass objects with my Paperweight and Millefiore designs, showing round paperweights full of circular forms. I was visiting a friend in America when I spotted a wonderful zany paperweight on her desk. The motifs weren't lined up in repeating circles like your average Venetian Murano paperweight; instead there was a delightful jumble of pastel glass "candies," as I call them. I asked to borrow that paperweight and sat down to paint out a repeat design that we have printed in many, many colorways, as it is a runaway bestseller.

Previous spread left, clockwise from top left: Kaffe's Spools print in the Contrast colorway; Kaffe's first hooked rug; a mosaic on the wall at Highland Stoneware Potteries in Scotland, by Kaffe and Brandon; Philip Jacobs's Curly Baskets fabric in the Delft colorway; Kaffe's Targets print in the Blue colorway; *Cups and Bowls* still life painting by Kaffe

Previous spread right: Kaffe's Tiddlywinks fabric in the Contrast colorway

BLUE SUZANI

Suzani (originally from the Persian word for needle, *suzan*) is a type of hand-embroidered textile traditionally from Central Asian countries including Kazakhstan, Tajikistan, and Uzbekistan, where it was a specialty in which the decorative panels would have been made by a bride and presented to her groom as part of her dowry. Suzanis often have colorful patterns, usually circular, formed on a woven cloth base, and embroidered traditionally in chain stitch with silk threads.

When I first moved to London in the 1960s, I got to know a wonderful carpet dealer who introduced me to the treasure trove of design ideas in ancient textiles. My eye focused on a brilliant red series of embroideries that featured a plethora of variations on circular motifs. Some of these were quite small, floral type circles of red on dark blue leafy branches. But the ones that appealed to the drama in me were the massive circles in scarlet on pale grounds. In my book *Passionate Patchwork*, I designed an autumnal version of a Suzani in golds and reds.

For this book, I went to the dark side, revisiting that layout with cool pools of teal, turquoise, leaf green, and warm lavender. I like seeing that snowball border in this cool palette with raspberry accents. The Royal Fan print in blue and dark plum echoes the circular theme.

The dark woven stripe and dark base prints help the colors to glow with the deep, low contrast. Quilting it was fun, with hand stitching in the large circles. These Central Asian embroideries, called *suzani*, have inspired me for years.

CIRCLE LOG CABIN

Anyone who has tuned into my designs might have noticed that circles play a huge role in my choice of subject matter. Beach balls, oranges, paint pots, targets, and poppies join the dance of pattern in this bright pastel quilt. Placing them in simple rows in log cabin style allowed me to show each scale of print to advantage. I think gray and shell pink are important here, creating a ground for the jolly bright pastels. It shouldn't be too hard to find a good variety of circular prints in your local shops or your stash to make this work.

I think the scales of prints from small- to very large-scale is important. You could do this in any theme: squares, paisleys, and stripes could all work and in a palette of your choosing. The contrasting polka dot binding is a good finishing note with Brandon's soft pink Onion Rings print as backing.

The center of this quilt, in my Beach Balls print, set the color theme, going through borders of various scales of circles culminating in the massive Target print spheres. I always find a mix of scales thrilling to play with. The Paint Pot print border and Oranges design bring a pleasing high-pastel warmth to the quilt. It reminds me of fruit markets in exotic places where you find every scale of circle, from lychees up to bulbous melons.

LACY CIRCLES

This checkerboard effect of circular images captured inside a square shape tickles me—I like the contrast of circles in squares. The pale "background" is the original colorway of Millefiore, my round, paperweight-inspired design containing all those glass candies that add such charm to old Venetian paperweights. It creates the lacy background for the stronger circular prints making up the darker elements in this quilt: curlicued snail shells, circular daisy forms, oranges, and stylized round flowers. Another idea is to create a version with fussy-cutting circular flowers for your darker checkerboard squares.

This is another one-patch quilt, made with 6-inch (15-cm) squares that create a delicate checkerboard effect. I used my Millefiore print in pastel every other square to create a lacy effect. All the other prints, including florals, are circular to create our theme. I love how seashells, flowers, oranges, and geometric prints create such a jolly variety of circles in a pastel mood with black and white spiciness.

Previous spread, clockwise from top left: Chrysanthemum plants in Amish country in the United States; yarn-bombed tree in South Africa; Kaffe's first hooked rug; Kaffe's Spot print in the White colorway; Brandon's Flower Dot print in the Stone colorway; spools in a weaver's studio; pomegranates on a market stall in Sicily; pumpkins; Kaffe's Button Mosaic print in the White colorway; hand-buttoned crochet hat by Kaffe; shell painting by artist Peter Plamondon; Brandon's Jumble print in the Rose colorway; needle-point shell carpet by Kaffe; a collection of buttons designed by Kaffe for Dill Buttons

SUNRISE

My Big Bang quilt is one of my favorite diamond layouts. I fell in love with exploding arrangements when I came across them in vintage quilt books, and I first used them in my book *Caravan of Quilts*. Since then, I've done exciting workshops on this pattern all over the world with stunning results. Revisiting this structure again for this book, with all circular motifs, was a joy. It is a real history of my past prints, some going years back. I've chosen a sunny, pastel palette, but you could of course choose any palette and stick to a theme like circles, flowers, stripes, or a mix of every motif. Just concentrate on getting the color balance as delicious as possible, occasionally incorporating a sharp contrast row. What a way to use that stash you've been hoarding.

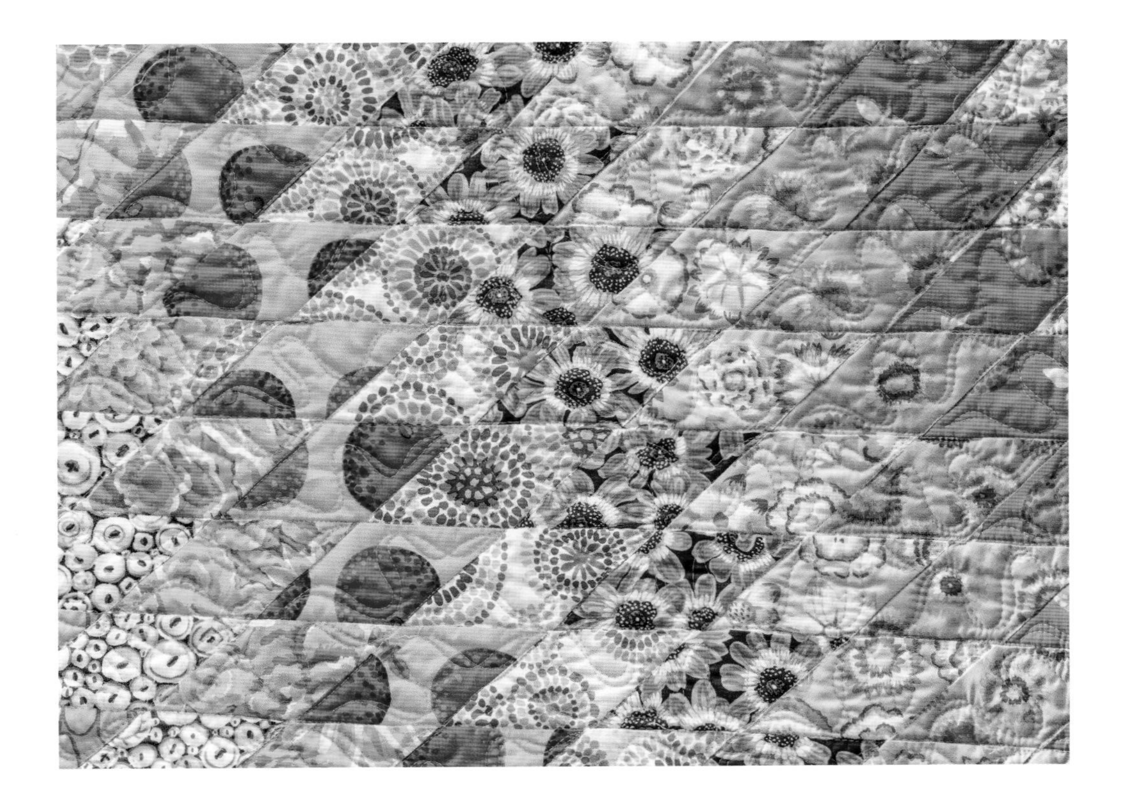

The bright sunny palette of this quilt glows against the painted shop front shutters on Aberfeldy Street.

BIKES

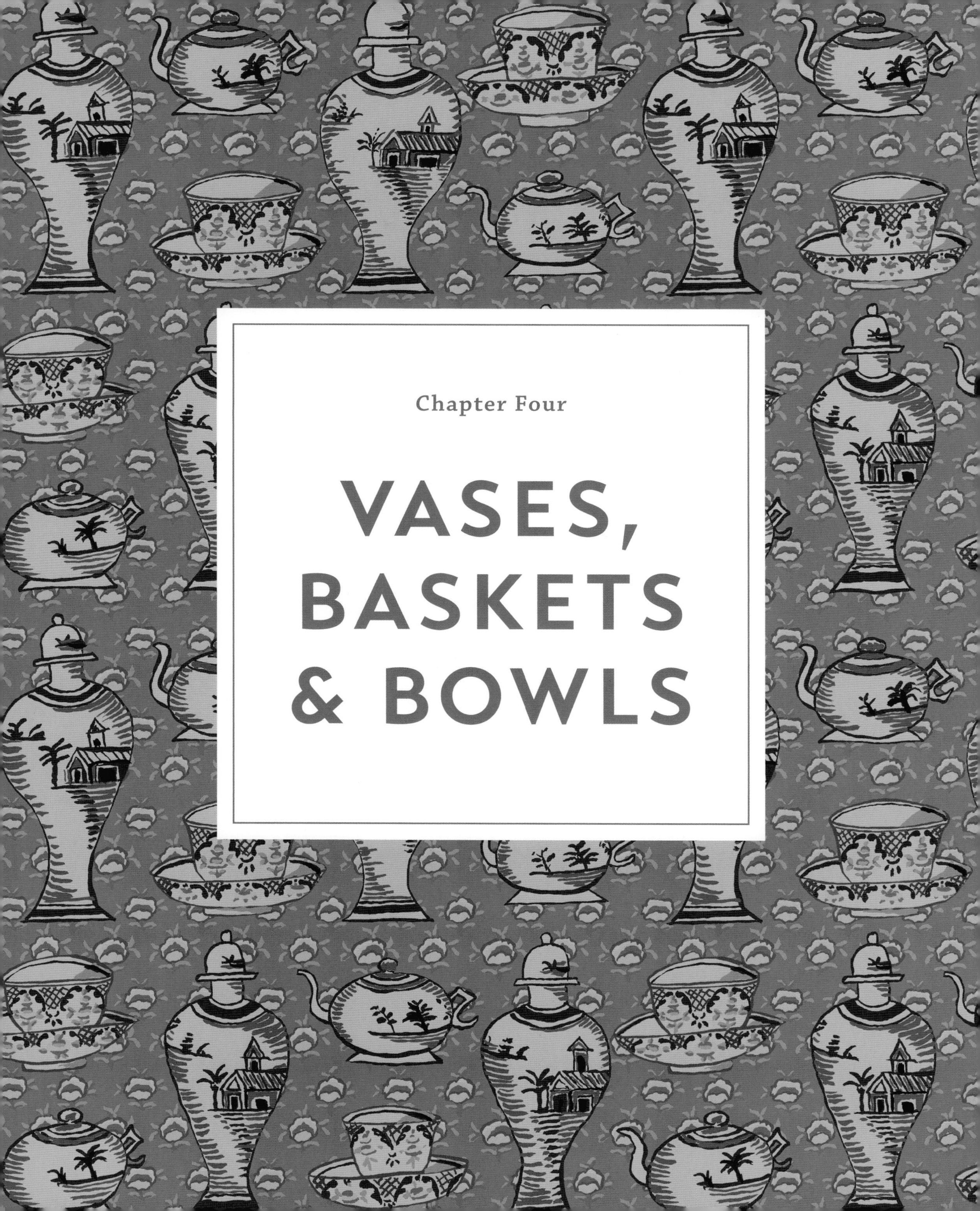

Chapter Four

VASES, BASKETS & BOWLS

Open Bowls still life painting by Kaffe, 2002

THIS IS A THEME that I return to often, mostly because I spot delightful examples of vases in decorative art on our world travels. I love how certain cultures see the charm in a decorative vase and use it in carpets, wall paintings, furniture painting, etc. From Scandinavia to India to Arab countries, I spot vases and baskets of flowers and capture that imagery directly into my prints, needlepoints, and collages. A lovely Persian carpet inspired me to create my Persian Vase print. The tiny vase and explosion of small sprays of flowers offer endless possibilities in patchwork.

I also love to paint bowls and teacups. Their pale interiors reflect a beautiful light, while the bodies of the bowls and cups often have delicate or bold patterns that are fun to paint and use as a patchwork theme. Rice Bowls is one of those bowl appliqué quilt designs I return to over and over, especially after teaching workshops on it and being inspired by all the variations my students come up with. Another quilt I'm fond of is the Lattice with Vases quilt I made for my book *Bold Blooms*. I find that graceful little vases or very large vases are a brilliant way to show off large-scale florals, as you can see in the Flowery Vases quilt on 156.

Pots on a Tray still life painting by Kaffe

Previous spread left, clockwise from top left: Kaffe's Persian Vase print in the Duck Egg colorway; Kaffe's Kirman print in the Green colorway; Kaffe's Cameo print in the Sky colorway, inspired by an Austrian painted cupboard; *Swirling Stripes* still life painting by Kaffe, 1998

Previous spread right: Kaffe's Delft Pots print in the Blue colorway

FLOWERY VASES

Big-scale, flowery Asian pots always get my attention in the museums and antique shops we visit on our travels. For this quilt, I picked Philip Jacobs's bold sunflower print, Van Gogh, one of the largest-scale florals in the collection, which set the mood for a spicy vase extravaganza. His Cactus Flower and Hokusai's Mums followed. The important thing to make these vessels come alive is to use large-scale prints for the vases. I placed them on blue-toned backgrounds to create a moody, cool statement. Cutting the flower prints so they are slightly off-center seems to give them a more realistic, three-dimensional feel.

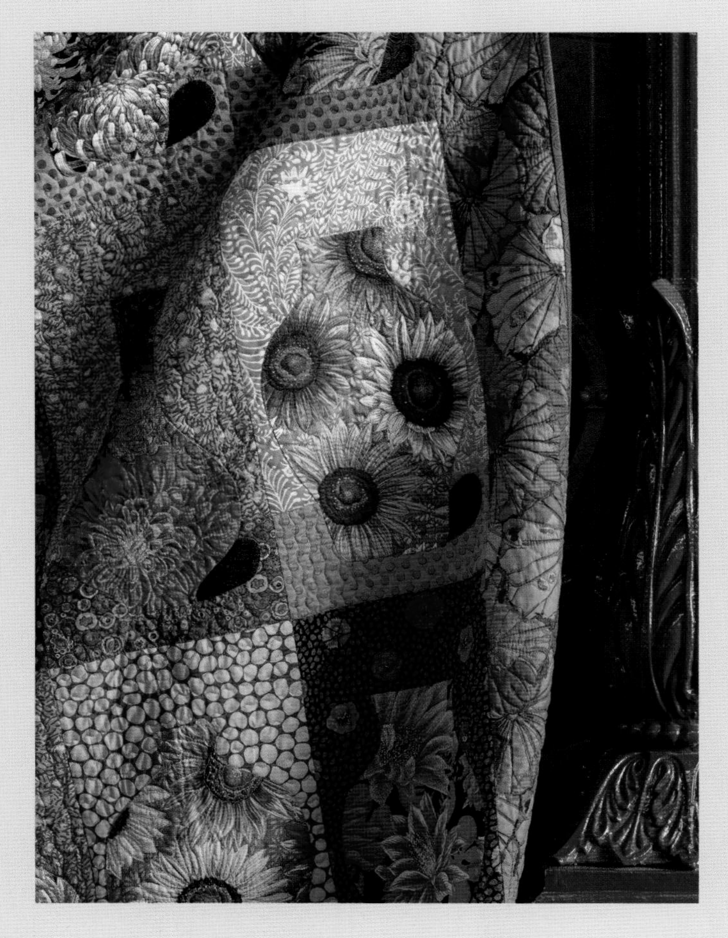

The painted gates at Smithfield Market make the colors in my Flowery Vases quilt really sing.

Next spread, clockwise from left: Basket of Flowers needlepoint by Kaffe, 2010; *Still Life with Pastel* sixteen-patch still life painting by Kaffe, photograph by Steve Lovi; metal pots in Morocco; Kaffe's Flower Basket print in the Duck Egg colorway; Kaffe's Striped Vase print in the Lavender colorway; *Geranium* still life painting by Kaffe, 1994; *White* still life painting by Peter Plamondon; detail from *Sunshine in the Mist* still life painting by Kaffe, 2020

FLOUR

AIN'T YOU GOT A VASE?

This quilt is a dip back into history to some early prints of mine that I felt were somewhat neglected, because I usually only have one season to show people how I'd play with any particular print. Vases are a theme that never fails to charm me when I find them all over the world, so of course it was inevitable that vases would turn up in several of my early prints.

This layout of simple, sashed squares gives me a happy kick each time I see it. I start with large-scale Stone Flower (originally designed as a wide quilt backing) in the center. Then the original-scale version of Stone Flower is the next border, and the outer borders are in Cameo, Delft Pots, and Persian Vase motifs in bright pastels. The sunny palette with contrasts of blue, burgundy, and magenta should light up any room. The original colorway of Paperweight for the sashing holds it all together. I hope you can find some similar prints in this variety of happy colors for this layout featuring vessels.

This quilt comes closest to my dream vision than any other in this book. I think what makes it work for me are the toile de Jouy elements that give a delicate line drawing at the center. The Paper Weight sashing in pastels creates a quiet life throughout the composition. The pastel tones in outer layers of prints add a sunny warmth. If you like this concept but have a collection of other subjects, any theme could be intriguing. Thinking about the color mood is important, so if you choose another group of images to highlight, be careful to keep them in the same color level. That could be dark, rich tones, high contrast of light and dark throughout, or bright jewel tones. Perhaps you are attracted to reproduction Civil War prints with their beautiful Victorian palette. Finding a large-scale print for your center is important. I chose my Stone Flower print in backing fabric-scale for my center, which contrasts with the normal-scale print in the first row of the quilt. So many of my colorways on those prints were soft enough to include here. The painted wall offsets it perfectly.

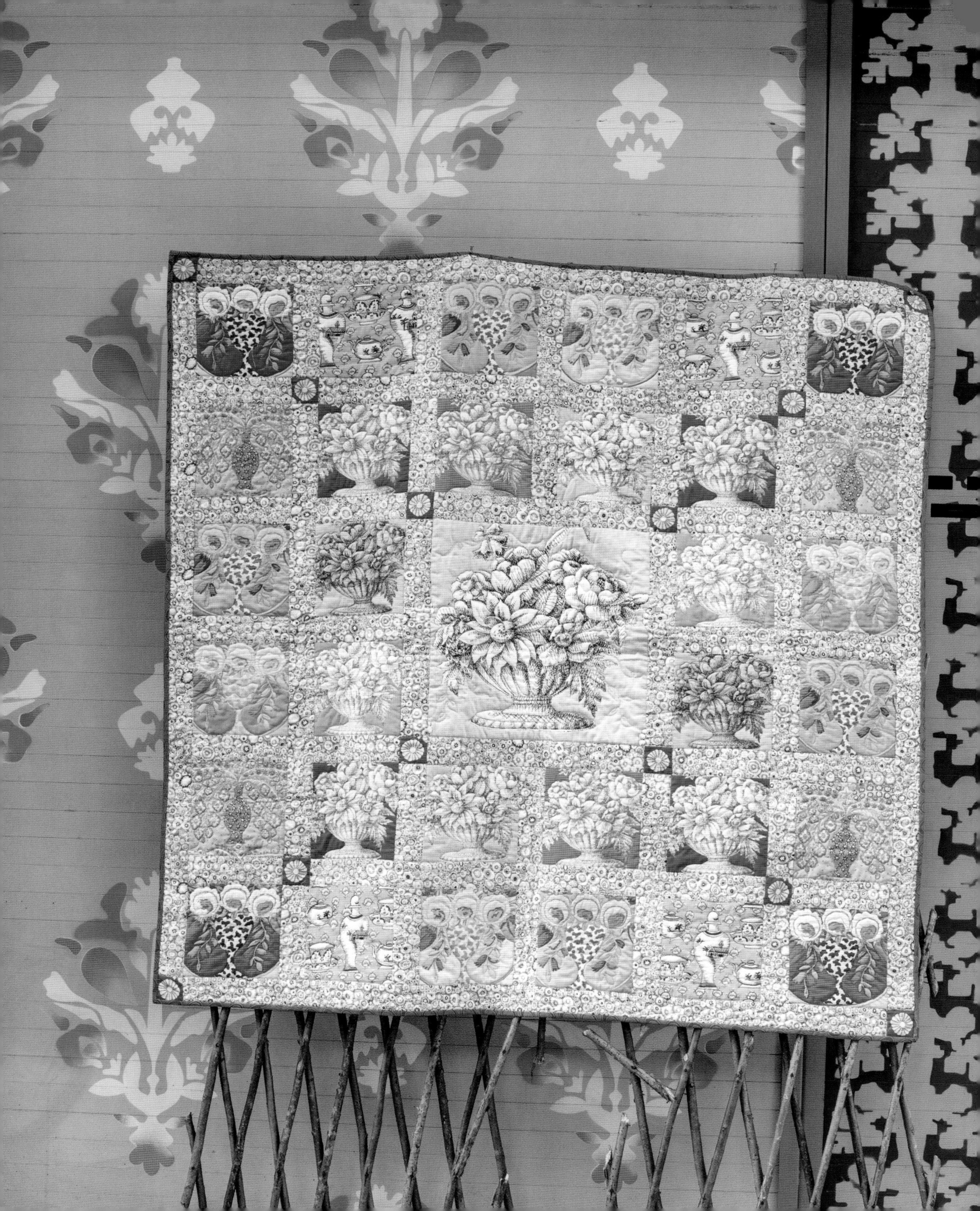

SCRAPPY RICE BOWLS

I find it strangely stimulating to revisit this study of bowls in so many moods through the years. I love the simple open roundness of it. As I put this particular scrappy version of it together, I thought of all the people around the world who have done startlingly original renditions of this layout, which inspired me to revisit it for this book. My versions have been more stylized, sticking to blue and white or some matching set of prints. Here, I've limited myself to round motifs in the prints, and because there is much more color variation, I kept the backgrounds and floors of each block as small-scale circular prints. It's important to have a big-scale graphic print for the exteriors of the bowls though, so it reads well.

We found the perfect mysteriously dark wall on Aberfeldy Street to highlight this quilt. My black and off-white Oranges print really comes to life on this background. Because it has such strong coloring, it has much sharper contrasts than I usually go for that are quite at home in this composition.

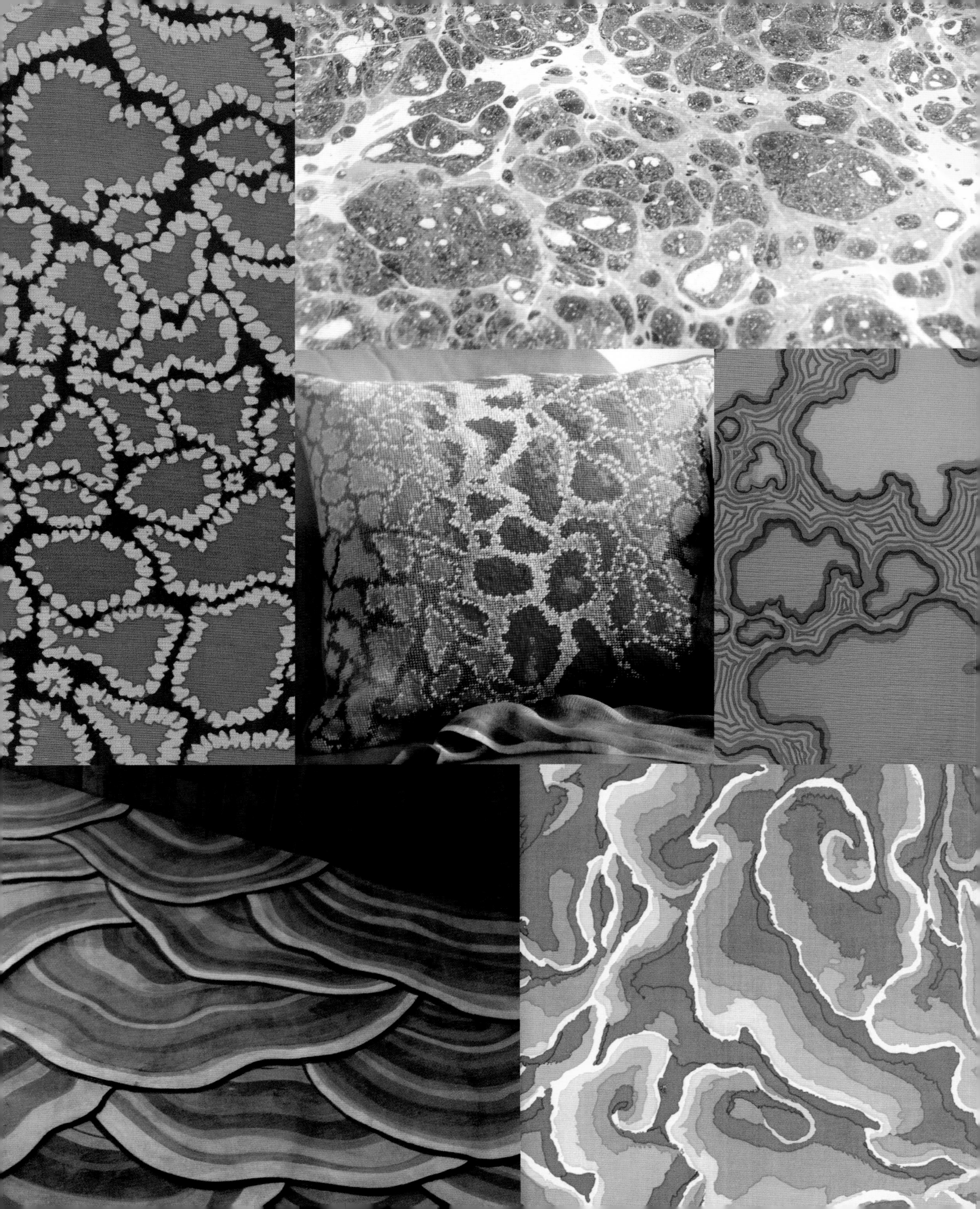

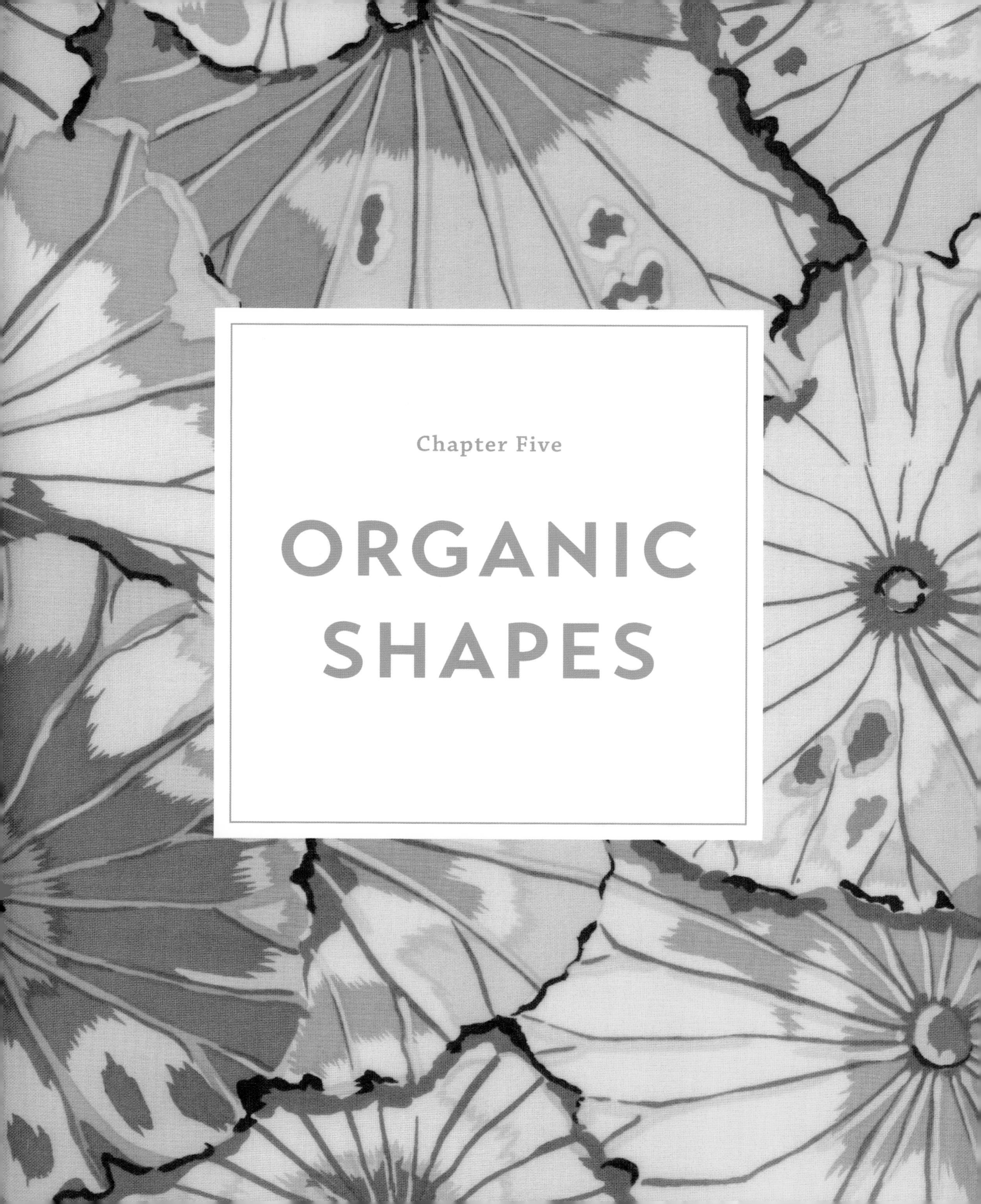

Chapter Five

ORGANIC SHAPES

Carved stone angel, Norway

NATURE'S MARKINGS had me transfixed from early childhood on the wild Big Sur coast of California—butterflies, fungi, bird feathers, and lichens were just some of the patterns that captivated my young creative mind. Later, when involved with the constant search for exciting color combinations, turtles, frogs, and snakes taught me as much as flowers did. But the real shock of pure color comes from under the earth, in the form of all those amazing minerals. My first visit to a natural history museum in Australia had me dancing with wonder and delight at the pinks, lavenders, turquoises, and lemon yellows under our feet.

This chapter celebrates all the weird and wonderful motifs that Brandon, in particular, is so drawn to. He has a go at his version of a snakeskin in his Animal print and his earlier Python print. His lava lamp–like prints, Splash and Aurora, and other textures are very effective when combined with other Kaffe Fassett Collective prints. Since Philip and I usually produce very detailed, painterly prints, Brandon's more graphic images bring a refreshing change of mood to the mix. Brandon's Onion Rings and Sharks Teeth prints in black and white provide a lively contrast to many of my quilts.

Philip Jacobs also flirts with pure organic shapes with great success. His Fungi print gave us wonderful organic stripes to play with in a few collections as I developed new colorways. In his Geode and Agate prints we get wonderfully rendered crystalline shapes that I love creating interesting colors for. His Feather design, with those lovely patterns found in so many feathers, has become a classic in our range. Philip placed a bold leopard print behind one of his florals to great effect, and his Classics Brassica print can pass as a marble texture in a quilt, as you can see in some of the quilts in this book.

Previous spread left, clockwise from top left: Brandon's Python print in the Black colorway; Brandon's Carmine Python needlepoint; marbled paper detail; Kaffe's Map print in the Red colorway; Kaffe's Wood Ear print in the Green colorway; inspiration for a scallop design

Previous spread right: Kaffe's Lotus Leaf print in the Jade colorway

ORGANIC LOG CABIN

Any follower of my designs will have observed I usually create quilt layouts that are traditionally balanced and symmetrical. But sometimes it's refreshing to break out, and my organic prints seemed to call out for something a bit looser in form. I particularly love my print inspired by undersea coral, and the scale and rhythm of it works so well here.

The free placement of organic prints was inspired by the Gee's Bend quilters of Alabama. Their wonderful quilts, sometimes made with found fabrics and work clothes, have freed up many quilters to be more expressive. Here, I've delved into my archive to find organic leaves, fungus, and florals in a warm palette. It's always great to have larger chunks of print to really show off the motifs. I feel the dotty, lacy textures and close tones of the prints help them to harmonize.

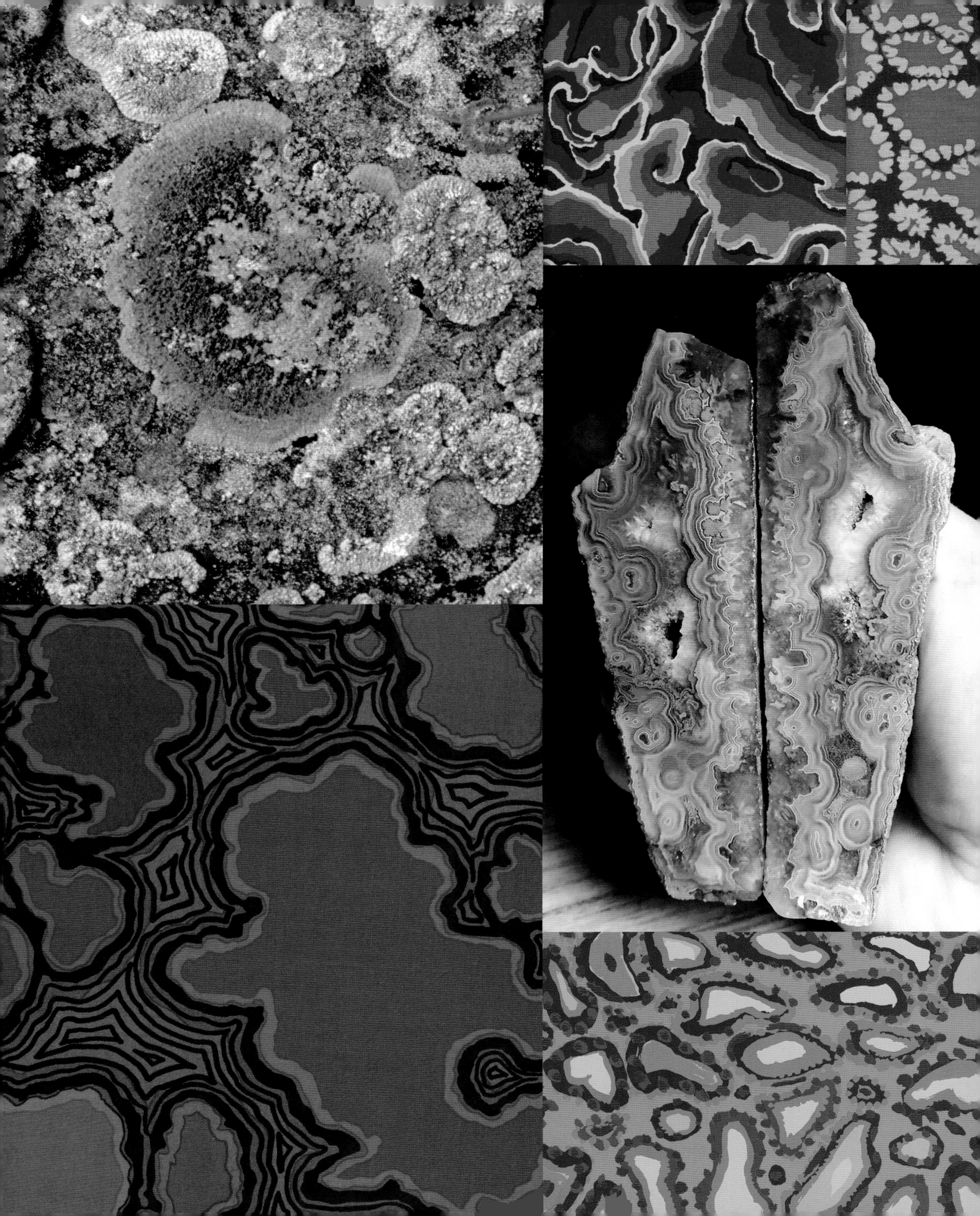

ORGANIC SEAHORSES

This is a structure I've always been drawn to in books and quilt shows. I loved doing my version in these dramatic, stony textures from Philip Jacobs's Agate and Brassica prints that read as a marble. The sharp contrasts make the structure come alive. When I was constructing this layout, I thought of all those Italian marble floors with inlaid designs that seem so three-dimensional that you almost lose your balance crossing over them.

This is a layout Brandon designed for our book *Quilts in Sweden*. His organic print, Animal, works best here along with Agate and Geode by Philip Jacobs. Organic Seahorses in these dramatic palettes would suit a man's room, not scaring him with too many florals!

Previous spread, clockwise from top left: Lichen, Scotland; Kaffe's Wood Ear print in the Red colorway; Brandon's Python print in the Black colorway; Painted Green Man mask by Kaffe; distressed door; wall painting, Australia; Kaffe's Lotus Leaf print in the Mauve colorway; Brandon's Animal print in the Orange colorway; Kaffe's Map print in the Dark colorway; colorful Agate, photo courtesy of Recep Imal; succulent mural by Kaffe and needlepoint frogs

Y OH Y

Here I've chosen mostly Philip Jacobs's Agate to create a marble-like structure you might find on an Italian floor. For powerful drama there is nothing like this Y formation, particularly when done at this level of contrast. The Brassica print becomes marble-like in this context.

It was fortuitous to find a panel of Rupert Spira tiles in a Y formation to show off our quilt. I like the way the round spiral shells contrast with the angular geometry in this one.

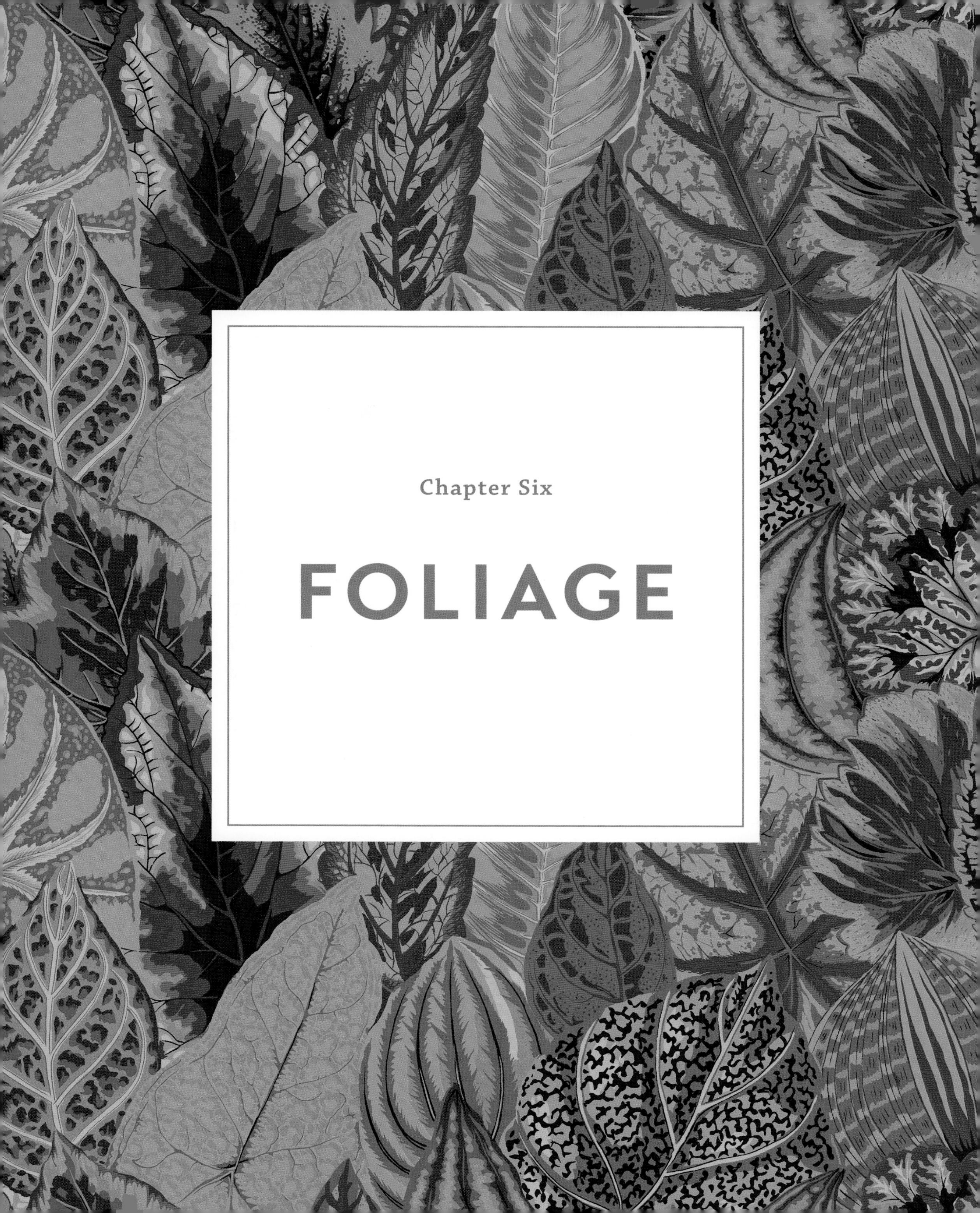

Chapter Six

FOLIAGE

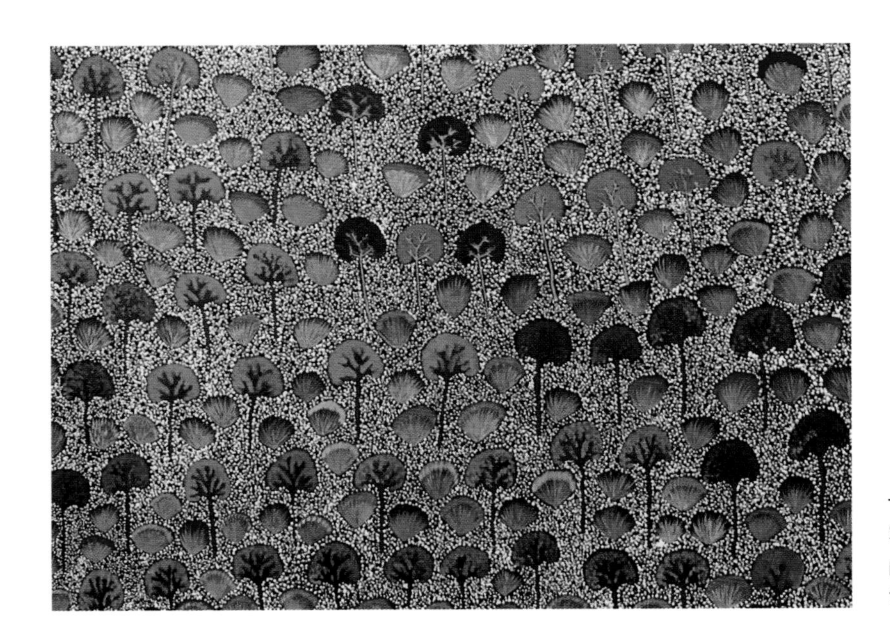

Study of painted leaves found in India

AFTER THE BRILLIANT high colors of flowers, the world of foliage may seem to take a back seat. But once you focus on the leaves of this planet, their vitality and vast variety of forms can make you swoon, and that's before we even start examining the extraordinary markings and colors they can exhibit. Brassica, a decorative cabbage print in the Kaffe Fassett Collective, is one of Philip Jacobs's most enduring prints. I love adding colors to this voluptuous pattern of veined leaves—it has been with our collection for years, and every year I find fresh ways to combine it with our newest prints. Sometimes it gives a very leafy effect; other times it can become a marble-like texture. Coleus is another very popular leafy print, with its striking pattern variations.

But I love humble geranium leaves, or my stylized forms like Vine and Embroidered Leaf, which were inspired by Shakespearean-era crewel work. England's Elizabethan era gave history beautiful embroidered leaves, which I captured in my Forest of Arden print. Of course, Autumn Leaves reminds me of my favorite season, when so much around us turns to burnished tones. I loved designing the appliqué panels for the autumn-inspired Leafy Appliqué quilt in *Bold Blooms*.

Lotus Leaf is another popular staple in our Classics range. I came up with this design after spotting a Japanese glazed garden stool in our yoga class. It had these large-scale circular leaves in warm pastels, and it was so memorable that I sketched it out when I came home. The design has remained in our collection for years.

In-progress detail of Kaffe's Vegetables long-stitch wall hanging

Previous spread left, clockwise from top left: One of Kaffe's first prints, Chard, in the Leafy colorway; Kaffe's Forest of Arden fabric in the Green colorway; Philip Jacobs's Maple Stream print in the Mauve colorway; collection of vegetable trinkets; Philip Jacobs's Geranium print in the Yellow colorway; leafy teapot

Previous spread right: Philip Jacobs's Coleus print in the Moss colorway

TUMBLING LEAVES

I must admit that the tumbling blocks pattern is one of my favorite quilt layouts. I've used it in knitting patterns and needlepoint cushions, and I've even painted tumbling blocks on floors. In this version, I keep all the dark sides of the blocks the same black and purple spot. The tops of the blocks are medium-tone prints, while the light sides are slightly lighter than the other prints. I like close tones on a piece like this, not harsh contrasts. (Though that can be exciting too, as we see in so many antique quilts.) I picked a rich smoldering palette (on the dark side) to go with the beautiful tile panels where we planned to photograph it. It was exciting to use all the leafy-motif prints—while keeping the level of deep color even—in this version.

You could use this layout to create so many different moods—bright pastels come to mind, with a medium-gray print as the dark side of the blocks. Any collection of motifs would do—leaves, flowers, geometrics, or spots and dotty prints perhaps. I've done one entirely in my shot stripes that was dazzling!

The fiery oranges of the Brassica print really sing out on this dark version of Tumbling Blocks done in leafy prints. The smoldering tiles make a good background.

SALAD DAYS

Salad Days is based on a snowball quilt I created for some earlier books. I love the mirror imaging in this layout, which isn't too obvious because carefully cutting different sections of the same prints creates subtle variations. I used my Banana Tree print in the center and let that set the palette of a fresh tossed salad. The shapes of the leafy prints remind me of folk art paintings from Haiti of jungle trees. The palette here is fresh and light-to-medium in the tonal level. The mirror imaging helps balance the snowball border.

This tiny jewel of a bathhouse in London showcases the leafy palette of my Salad Days quilt to perfection. Previous spread, clockwise from top left: Carved pottery vase; fallen leaves, Boca Raton, Florida; Philip Jacobs's Geranium fabric in the Yellow colorway; autumn foliage; Kaffe's embroidered Shawl print in the Red colorway; *Spring* by Giuseppe Arcimboldo, 1563; Brandon's flower-on-leaves photo; succulents, California; tiled steps, Amsterdam; mammoth leaf, Singapore; Kaffe's Forest of Arden print in the Grey colorway

Chapter Seven

SPOTS, SPRAYS & SMALL FLORALS

Enamel cup and saucer, Victoria and Albert Museum, London

THOUGH I LOVE beyond love big, bold blooms, there is an undeniable charm in small flowers: Forget-me-nots, snowdrops, and pinks spring to mind. There is definitely magic in the miniature. When I was a small child, I delighted in finding wild strawberries, which are a dollhouse version of the cultivated strawberries we see in every supermarket. The punch of their sharp, wild flavor equals the effect a tiny smattering of forget-me-nots, for instance, can have on a flower arrangement. The world of Asian carpets and Indian miniature paintings are also chock-full of sprays of tiny star-like flowers. The Slavic countries often feature repeats of small flowers in wall paintings and embroidered dance costumes.

Polka dots have become a cornerstone of the Kaffe Fassett Collective, and we have used our wide range of colorways in masses of quilts designed over the past fifteen or so years that we've had this useful design in our Classics range. There is something intriguing about a surface of color punctuated by a small motif like a dot. It was a great way to get more pools of color into my Classics range of prints. I of course love large-scale polka dots, like a fabric I did titled Paint Pots, which is seen in the Circle Log Cabin quilt, or the Oranges print, which is basically a big polka dot. Brandon's Jumble design is an organic, medium-scale print I use constantly in my quilts.

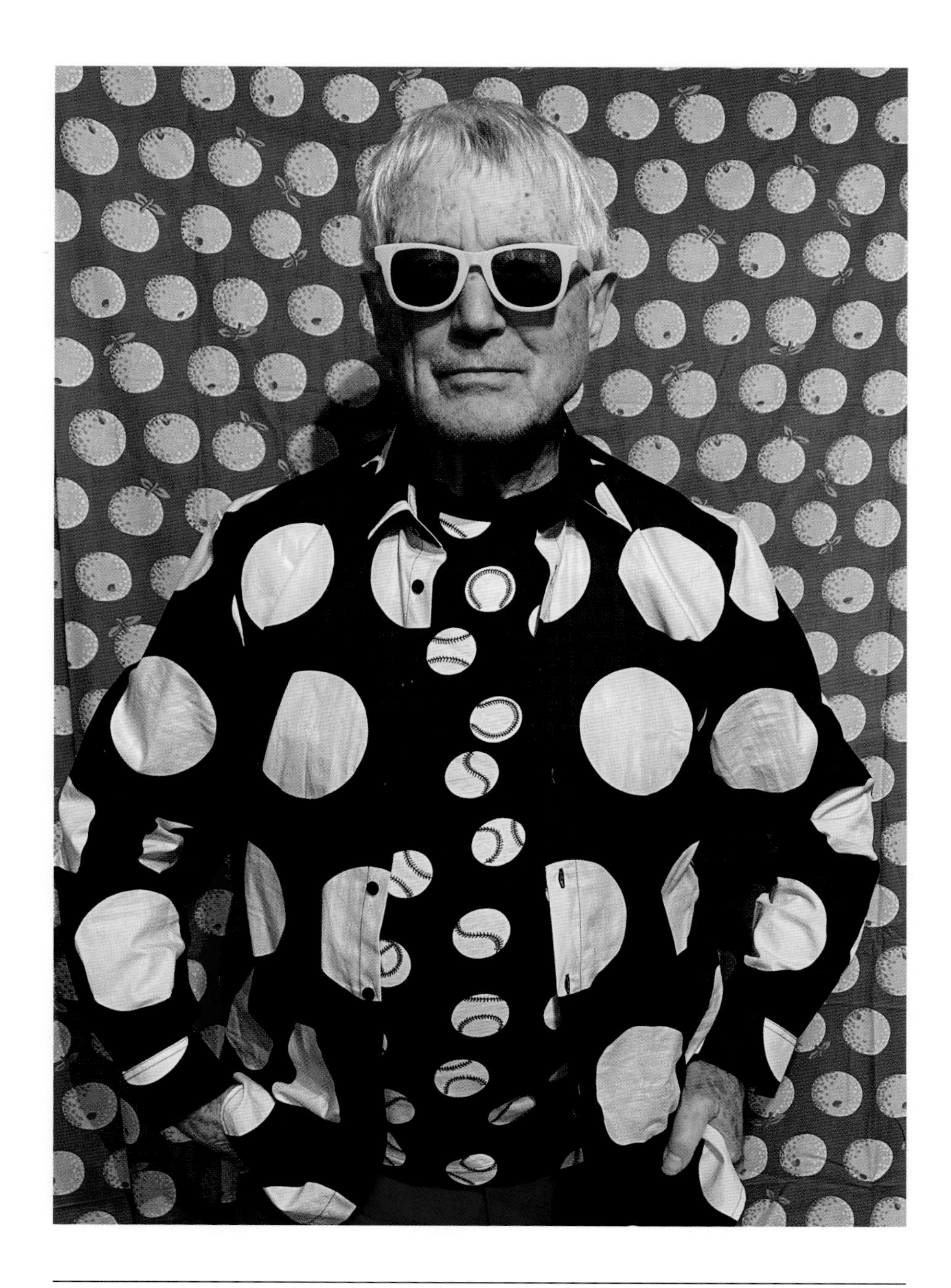

Kaffe in spots and baseballs against his Oranges fabric in the Lavender colorway

Previous spread left, clockwise from top left: Oriental carpet; Cherry Blossom Jar, hand-knitted cushion by Kaffe; Kaffe's Zinnia print in the Crimson colorway; Kaffe's Persian Garden print in the Grey colorway; Chelsea Flower Show, London; knitted swatch by Kaffe inspired by a makeup box; Basket of Robin's Eggs, needlepoint by Kaffe

Previous spread right: Brandon's Bubble Stripe print in the Purple colorway

MONKEY WRENCH

I found this "monkey wrench" layout on a not very inspiring quilt in one of my vintage books. It was fun to see this lively pattern come to life in my dramatic, deep-colored version. It needed contrast, but a glowing set of rich blues in medium-to-dark tones did the trick. I've used only small dotty and floral prints, but this quilt could be made in a handsome set of solids or other small prints. Highly contrasting black and white could be exciting. The vigorous profile of this block in this quilt is made more distinct by the use of medium-to-small prints. I kept the palette dark to make the blues and purples glow. If you want even more contrast, try black and white prints or pastels with dark prints on every other one. It's a good way to use spots and small florals.

The smoldering tones of Rupert Spira's block tiles made a gorgeous setting to show off the glowing blues of my Monkey Wrench quilt.

SUGAR CUBES

I love my dotty prints, so it was only a matter of time before I brought them all together in this confection of squares. Keeping the palette in soft pastels, I ended up with a sweet concoction. I like this square-on-square format and have done several versions of it over the years. This variation on the log cabin block in contrasting squares has always appealed to me, and when the blocks are made of bright pastels, black and white spots, and dappled prints, they really vibrate for me. This same layout could be made in much higher contrast to exciting effect.

I called this Sugar Cubes because the spotty prints were such a sweet pastel palette. But it could equally be called confetti, as it reminds me of the celebratory scatter of multicolored confetti at a wedding. I was after a subtle, almost merging here, but in that distinct log cabin shape with defined squares. The use of small- to medium-scale prints is important, which seems to be what most quilters are drawn to. I look forward to seeing what different moods you come up with for this fizzy concept.

Previous spread, clockwise from top left: Mosaic armchair by Candace Bahouth; bowl on a tea towel; Count Your Blessings needlepoint panels; fans in a Spanish market; Kaffe's needlepoint slippers for Ehrman Tapestry; non-slip pavement treatment; Persian tiles; stone bottles, Victoria and Albert Museum, London; photograph of tulips by Steve Lovi; South African donkey; spotted flowers

TICKLED PINK

For this sizzling treat, another six-inch square piece, I grabbed every red-to-pink dot and small print I could lay my hands on for a blushing number. Brandon's Jumble is one of our Classics and is, as you can see, playful and useful. It appears in many quilts in this book. Here, it's positively fizzy. I could have called this quilt Pink Champagne because the whole effect is quite bubbly. The pink palette has a glowing effect on the quilt, but it could be made very effectively in strong contrasts like blue, or black and white.

I loved delving into my archive to find every print that had small sprays of flowers or dotty motifs in a high rosy palette. This concept could be done in any series of motifs you fancy and in any color mood. I'd love to see it done in a majority of black and white prints with other high contrast prints in the same theme. All plaids or paisleys or animal prints could make gorgeous quilts that keep the viewer intrigued. I chose a border that keeps the action going with Brandon's Jumble print at the corners, to create the enclosing feeling a border can sometimes give a quilt. The consistent square blocks make you more aware of the different scales and tones in the collection of prints.

I've always loved pink. When I went to India, I found a whole continent that felt the same way, and I applauded Diana Vreeland (then editor in chief of *Vogue*) for saying "pink is the navy blue of India." Here, I've gathered every medium-scale dotty and flowery print in warm pastels to create this blushing ripple of happiness. Using the one-patch, six-inch squares seemed fine, as the differing scales and tones of the prints do the rest of the work. I chose a well-defined medium print for my border to keep the action going.

Chapter Eight

FLOWERS

Embroidered panel, Jordan

FLOWERS, particularly in English gardens, are a great instructor on the power of color. The elegant planting that uses high pastels with silver-leafed plants creates a delicate mood in so many gardens in England. But I also love the bright contrasts I find in bouquets in Bali, say, or the fabric prints and embroideries I find in decorative arts museums the world over. Flowers are the timeless motif that has delighted people from the earliest times, and as anyone who knows my work sees, it has been my dominant inspiration.

This page: Glorious Bouquet flower panel. Photo courtesy of Ehrman Tapestry

Previous spread left, clockwise from top left: Philip Jacobs's Cactus Flower design in the Tawny colorway; one of Kaffe's Flower Panels in long stitch; *Rose in Turquoise* Vase painting by Kaffe; *Dahlias in Pink Teapot* painting by Kaffe; Kaffe's Shakespearean Flowers on the Sand needlepoint cushion, 2015; Philip Jacobs's Flora print in the Dark colorway; Kaffe's Mexican Rose needlepoint for Ehrman Tapestry

Previous spread right: Philip Jacobs's Japanese Chrysanthemum print in the Scarlet colorway

BLOOMERS

This quilt is a celebration of the flowers of every scale in my prints. Because there is such a maelstrom of detail, it's important to pick flowers with a clear profile. Often in my workshops, people will pick blooms that are merging with their backgrounds and are not sharply defined—not good in a piece like this. I also think it helps to have a predominant color or two in your choices. I chose a bright yellow, lime, and orange with accents of magenta and pink. This concept could be done with any subject matter: Animals, graphic geometrics, leaves, or human faces could make exciting, obsessive works like this. If you go for flowers, as I have, do take care to have some prints, like the sunflowers, that really establish your theme with their dramatic bursting shapes. This concept could be even more livable within soft antique tones and pearly grays.

Detail of some of the fussy-cut flowers in Bloomers

FLOWERS IN THE MIST

This quilt plays with my favorite camouflage effect. I made an effort to find florals in color moods that would almost merge into my white colorway of Philip's Brassica surrounding each block. Brandon's Flower Net print makes a good sashing that doesn't dominate or enclose the blocks too much. Often in this book, I am reaching for clearly defined blocks in my quilts, but here I really wanted to lose my flowers in a detailed background. I thought of Indian paintings of subjects on top of strongly marbled paper. Using Brassica's cabbage-like leaves, I dropped in flowers that almost merge. I kept the palette gray in mood with a few high pastels. The sashing is a lacy print in black, blue, and white that adds to the mistiness.

The squares on this lattice tile panel echo the square-on-square structure of our Flowers in the Mist.

Previous spread, clockwise from top left: Japanese kimono flowers from Kaffe's collection; London petunias; Kaffe in front of a mural in the United States; close-up of a tin flower tree in China; tin flower tree in China; Rose named 'Kaffe Fassett'—what an honor! Kaffe's long-stitch cushion made for the Royal Shakespeare Company's production of *As You Like It*; flower-decorated cakes in Texas; Kaffe's Pansy rag rug; needlepoint chair seat made by Kaffe

FLORAL CHECKERBOARD

I found this snowball, one of my favorite traditional layouts, in a vintage quilt book. It was done in mostly solid colors, and I thought it would be a good vehicle for circular, large-scale florals. Often in my quilts, I play with a tonal story, keeping the prints all in shades of a particular color mood. But this quilt longed to play with contrast, so I used small-scale prints between the fussy-cut large blooms and sashed it in a circular daisy print. I tried to keep the strong contrast going that the vintage quilt had. To emphasize the large-scale blooms in this quilt, I used small, more tonal prints on each block to contrast with my flowers. It was unusual and fun for me to use more contrast than usual, often pitting cool tones against hotter ones, and with definite contrast in scale.

The deep, smoldering tiles on Rupert Spira's tile panels make our Floral Checkerboard quilt really glow. I could see this quilt in a bedroom with leafy green wallpaper and flowery cushions.

QUILT INSTRUCTION INDEX

PART TWO

INSTRUCTIONS

BORO

I tried to use only my darkest woven stripes for this quilt, so some almost become invisible. I used fabric glue to lightly hold the raw edge rectangles in place, then hand-stitched my long, Kantha-style stitches in contrasting thread through the rectangles.

FINISHED SIZE

Approximately 56 × 80 inches (142 × 220 cm). The exact measurements are not essential. A larger size can become harder to manage, but going smaller to make a shawl or a scarf works beautifully.

FABRIC CHOICES

The fabrics used in the original are Woven Stripes from the Kaffe Fassett Collective.

3½ yards (3.2 m) Wide Stripe Ink
½ yard (46 cm) each of
- Wide Stripe Fjord
- Wide Stripe Kiwi
- Wide Stripe Peat
- Wide Stripe Russet
- Narrow Stripe Midnight
- Narrow Stripe Seaweed
- Narrow Stripe Cocoa

¼ yard (23 cm) Wide Stripe Moss

Backing:

3½ yards (3.2 m) Lotus Leaf Purple

NOTIONS

Safety pins
Assortment of brightly colored Aurifil 12 wt threads
Bohin #7 or #9 Darner needles
Bohin glue stick

PREPARING THE BACKING

Remove the selvages from the Lotus Leaf Purple. Cut the remaining yardage in half so that you have 2 panels measuring approximately 41 × 57 inches (104 × 145 cm). Sew the two panels together lengthwise, making a large panel measuring approximately 81 × 57 inches (206 × 145 cm).

PREPARING THE BACKGROUND

Remove the selvages from the Wide Stripe Ink, leaving you with one length measuring approximately 40 × 81 inches (101.5 × 210 cm). Cut the remaining yardage lengthwise to get two panels measuring approximately 20 × 41 inches (51 × 104 cm). Sew together end to end to make one piece measuring approximately 20 × 81 inches (51 × 206 cm). Sew this piece to the larger one, making a background that measures approximately 59 × 81 inches (150 × 210 cm). Trim this background to the exact same size as the backing.

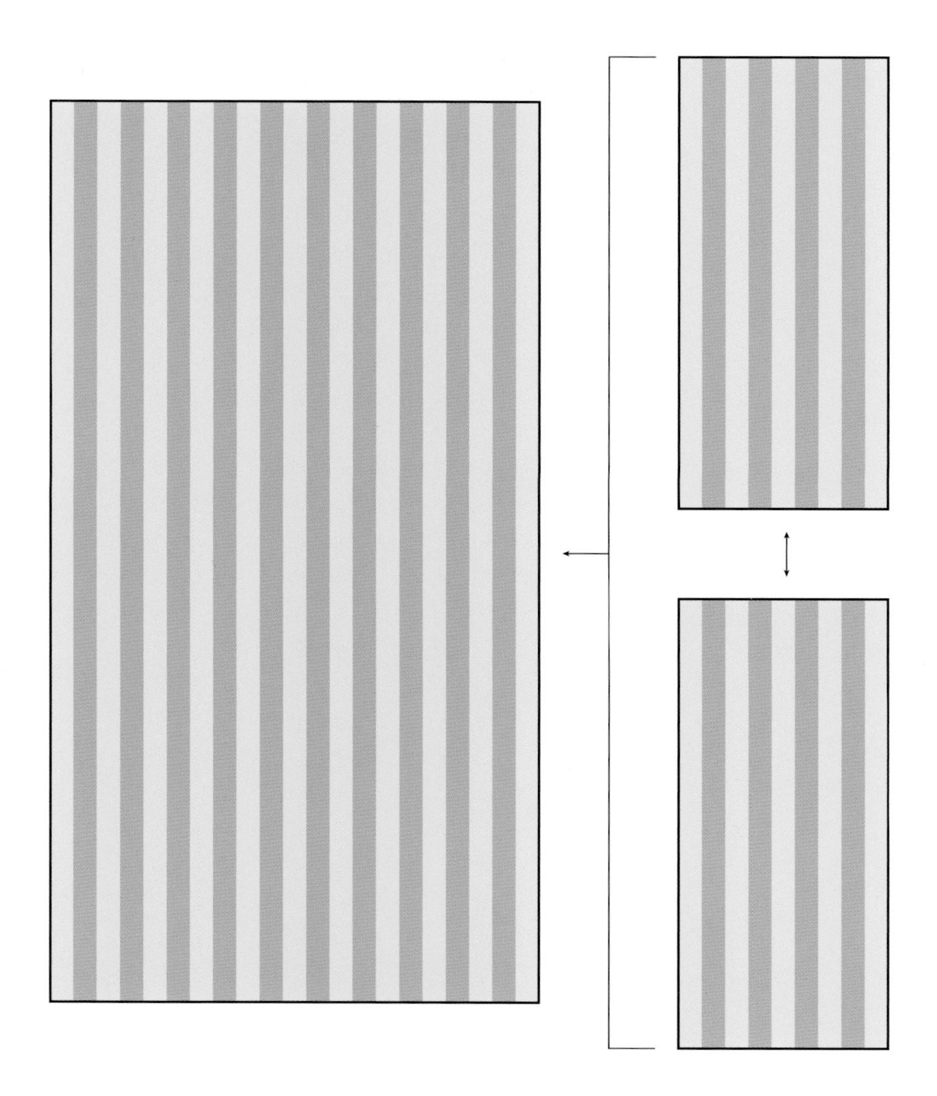

ASSEMBLING

With right sides together, sew the background panel to the backing panel along the edges, three-fourths of the way around. Turn right side out. Press flat, turn opening edges in, and topstitch closed.

Cut various widths and lengths of the other striped fabrics and arrange these patches until you have a harmonious and pleasing effect.

Using safety pins, attach the patches all the way through to the backing. Using the glue stick, lightly tack the patches to the background.

FINISHING

Take long visible running stitches lengthwise through all the layers. Anchor the beginning and ending knots between the two layers.

CORRUGATED

Note: Three of the quilts in this book share a truly timeless theme—the ubiquitous one-patch—so we have combined the cutting and assembly instructions for Corrugated, Tickled Pink, and Lacy Circles.

I've had a lifelong love affair with bold stripes. I spot them everywhere on my travels, so doing this quilt was a great enjoyment for me. I went through my stash and current collections to find every stripe I could with a medium-to-dark toning, so here are mostly two-color stripes with my multitoned, organic Jupiter stripes, my Shirt Stripes and Marquee Stripe, and a multicolored stripe I created a few collections ago. I've even included a few of Tula Pink's two-colored stripes.

Think of the fun you can have finding all sorts and scales of stripes to do your version. You could use floral stripes or paisley stripes along with graphic bold stripes from any sort of collection. I would keep the color balance to all dark or all medium tones, or dark smolders. Of course, the most actively exciting of all would be contrast stripes, so each stripe would have light and dark elements that would all hang together and give you a lively result.

There is something about this simple layout of 5½-inch (14-cm) squares that helps the eye see the variation of scale and tone in your collection of stripes. Using some printed and some woven stripes gives variety. Keeping the work all in the same size squares helps the viewer to see the subtle variations.

Try arranging the patches on a design wall before committing to a single stitch. The wonderful thing about using a flannel design wall is that the squares cling to the flannel, and moving them around is so simple.

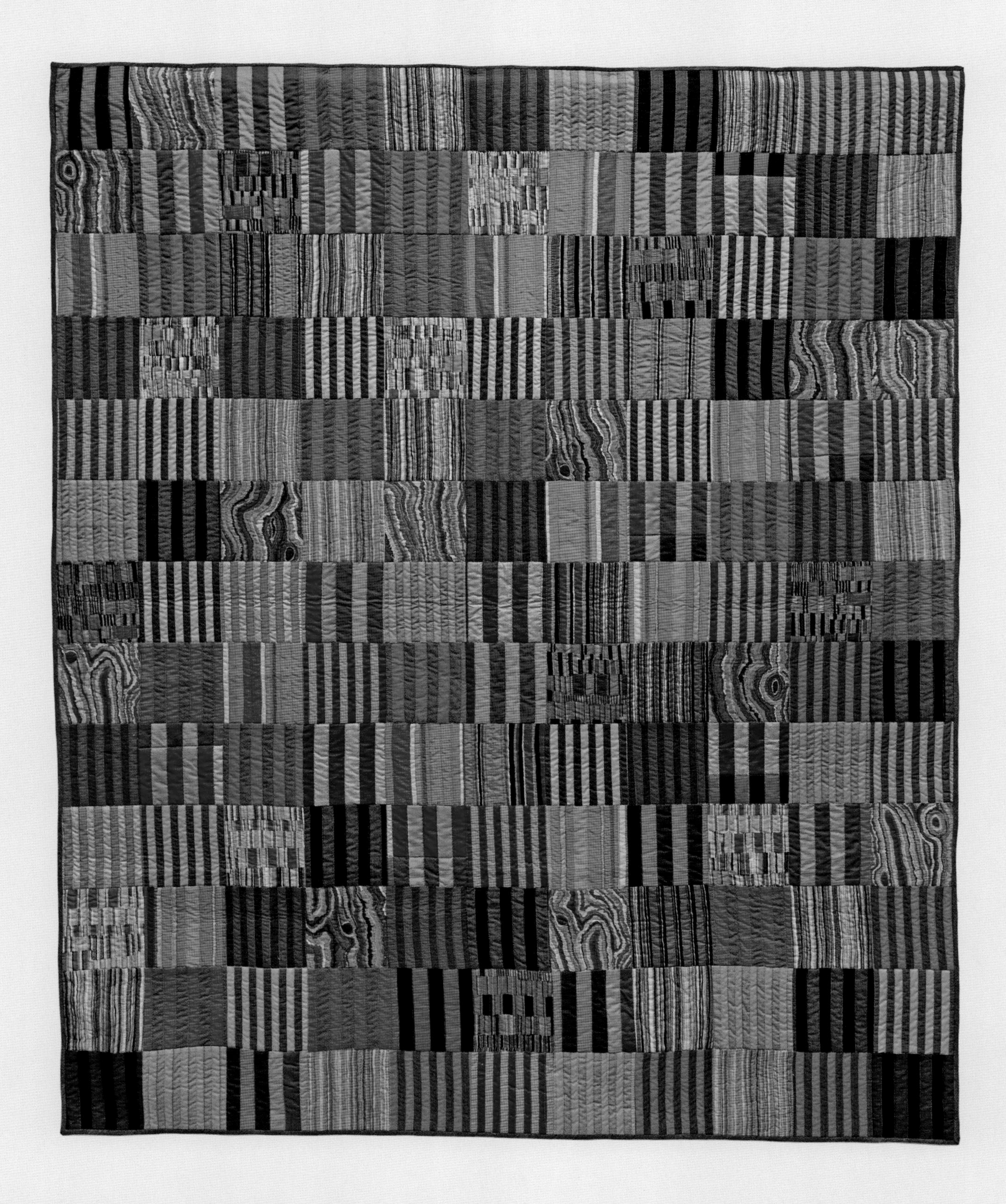

FINISHED SIZE

60½ × 71½ inches
(153.5 × 181.5 cm)
This one-patch design uses 5½-inch (14-cm) finished squares, but it can be made with any size square.

FABRIC CHOICES

Scraps or ¼ yard (23 cm) of a variety of woven stripe or printed stripe fabrics in medium-to-dark tones. Some of the fabrics used here are Jupiter Blue and Red, plus Woven Stripes Peat, Embers, Fjord, Mallard, Cocoa, Seaweed, Heather, Chestnut, and Moss.

PLEASE NOTE: The names and colorways listed in this book are selections from the Kaffe Fassett Collective. Some of these fabrics are readily available; others are no longer in print. If one fabric is no longer available, we discourage you from hunting the world for it. Instead, make these patterns your own with selections from your own stash or local shops!

Backing:

4 yards (3.7 m) printed fabric, preferably one with a stripe theme.

Binding:

¾ yard (68.5 cm) Woven Stripe Moss
Please see page 123
for cutting and assembly instructions.

CUTTING

Cutting for the center of all three quilts:
Cut all squares 6 × 6 inches (15 × 15 cm) from an assortment of fabrics.
For Corrugated, cut a total of 143 squares.
For Tickled Pink, cut a total of 120 squares.
For Lacy Circles, cut 50 Millefiore squares, 22 Mosaic Circles squares, and 71 scrappy squares, for a total of 143 squares.

LACY CIRCLES

Any collection of circles could be used for this concept. You could also create a layout using higher contrast, really emphasizing the checkerboard. Every other square in the center is Millefiore Pastel, and every other square along the edges is Mosaic Circles White.

FINISHED SIZE

71½ × 82½ inches
(181.5 × 210 cm)

FABRIC CHOICES

1½ yards (137 cm) Millefiore Pastel
¾ yard (68.5 cm) Mosaic Circles White
Scraps or ¼ yard (23 cm) of a variety of gray or grayed pastel fabrics, all with a circular theme and all light- or medium-toned. These can be flowers that are round, or strong graphic patterns with circles. Some of the fabrics we used are Onion Rings Black, Lucy Grey and Pink, Flower Dot Stone, Guinea Flower White, Oranges Pink, Embroidered Flower Contrast, Tiddlywinks Contrast, and Spiral Shells Blue and Multi.

Backing:
5 yards (4.6 m) of a print with a circular theme

Border:
2⅛ yards (2 m) of a large dotty fabric

Binding:
¾ yard (68.5 cm) Onion Rings Black or a stripey black and white print

Instructions apply to Corrugated, Tickled Pink, and Lacy Circles. Corrugated has no border. Follow the instructions that follow for the borders for Tickled Pink and Lacy Circles.

TICKLED PINK

Scale is important here, and so is the level of tone. If you pick darker prints, be sure no light ones stop the movement. High contrast on all the prints, like black and white, could be exciting, or all delicate pastels. Pick a lively print for a border.

FINISHED SIZE

66 × 77 inches
(167.5 × 195.5 cm)

FABRIC CHOICES

Scraps or ¼ yard (23 cm) of a variety of deep pink, red, or orange/red fabrics, all with a dotty theme and all medium toned. Some of the fabrics we used are Garlands Red, Tiddlywinks Red, Flower Dot Aqua, Roman Glass Lavender, Millefiore Mauve, Wisteria Red and Grey, and Jumble Bubblegum, Tangerine, and Rose.

Backing:
5 yards (4.6 m) of a mostly red print fabric

Border:
1½ yards (137 cm) Garlands Red or a deep red print with a dotty theme

Binding:
¾ yard (68.5 cm) Jumble Bubblegum or a print with a pink/red dot
Please see page 123 for cutting and assembly instructions.

CUTTING

Cut 143 squares 6 × 6 inches (15 × 15 cm) from an assortment of fabrics.

Borders for Tickled Pink:

Cut 7 strips measuring 6 inches (15 cm) wide, selvage to selvage. Remove the selvages, sew end to end, then cut 2 lengths measuring 66½ inches (169 cm). Cut 2 more lengths measuring 55½ inches (141 cm).

Cut four identical squares measuring 6 × 6 inches (15 × 15 cm) for the border corners.

Borders for Lacy Circles:

Cut 2 lengths measuring 6 × 72 inches (15 × 180 cm) and 2 lengths measuring 6 × 61 inches (15 × 155 cm).

For the backings and bindings:

For Corrugated backing, cut 2 lengths measuring approximately 41 × 69 inches (104 × 175 cm). Remove selvages and sew together, making a backing that measures approximately 82 × 69 inches (2 m × 175 cm).

For Corrugated binding, cut the Woven Stripe Moss on the bias, 2½ inches (6 cm) wide. Make at least 270 inches (701 cm) of binding.

For Lacy Circles backing, cut 2 lengths measuring approximately 41 × 90 inches (104 × 244 cm). Remove selvages and sew together, making a backing approximately 82 × 90 inches (2.2 × 2.4 m).

For Lacy Circles binding, cut 8 strips measuring 2½ inches (6 cm) wide, selvage to selvage. Remove selvages and sew end to end.

For Tickled Pink backing, cut 2 lengths approximately 41 × 85 inches (104 × 216 cm). Remove selvages and sew together, making a backing approximately 80 × 85 inches (2.2 × 2.16 m). Trim to approximately 74 × 85 inches (188 × 216 cm).

For Tickled Pink binding, cut 8 strips 2½ inches (6 cm) wide, selvage to selvage. Remove selvages and sew end to end.

ASSEMBLING

Using a design wall, arrange the squares. Sew the squares into rows. Sew the rows together.

For Corrugated, make sure your stripes run vertically. There are 11 squares in each row. There are 13 rows.

For Tickled Pink, there are 10 squares in each row. There are 12 rows.

For Lacy Circles, there are 11 squares in each row. There are 13 rows.

For Tickled Pink border, sew the longer lengths to the sides. Sew corners on each end of the shorter lengths, then sew to the top and to the bottom.

For Lacy Circles border, sew 2 border lengths to the sides. Sew the corners on each end of the shorter lengths, then sew to the top and bottom.

FINISHING

Press. Layer top, batting, and backing. Baste. Quilt Corrugated using a deep neutral thread. Follow the stripes in each patch. Quilt Lacy Circles using a pale gray thread and meander making circles. Quilt Tickled Pink using a red thread and meander throughout.

Trim. Bind.

This illustration shows a basic construction technique for a one-patch pattern with no border. Please follow the instructions above to add a border for Tickled Pink and Lacy Circles.

The 11 x 13-block pattern shown here applies to Corrugated and Lacy Circles. Tickled Pink requires a pattern of 10 × 12 blocks.

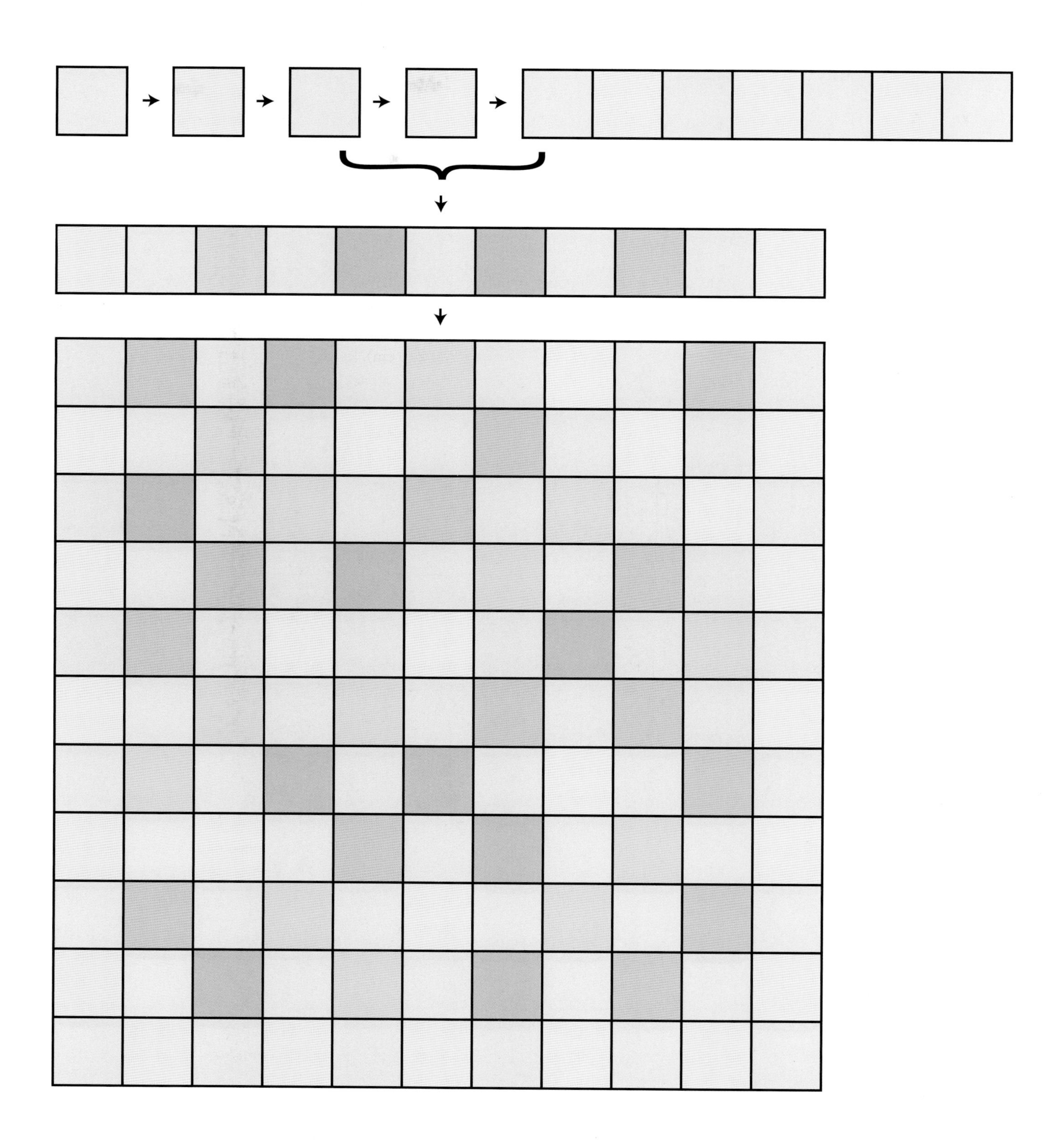

STRIPED SQUARES

Keeping your color mood consistent is the most important thing with Striped Squares. I've used all medium-toned pastels, but you could use all darks, or all high-contrast stripes for a jazzier version.

FINISHED SIZE

45 × 72½ inches
(114 × 184 cm)

FABRIC CHOICES

All but one of the fabrics are Woven Stripes from the Kaffe Fassett Collective. The small black and white stripe is a printed fabric (Creased, from the Kaffe Fassett Collective), but it could be any small-scale black-and-white stripe.
This is a scrappy quilt. It is not necessary to place each fabric as in the original. Choose your favorites to be used in the bigger blocks.

The amounts given are just guidelines. Add more colors if you wish!

½ yard (46 cm) each Woven Stripe in Burn, Blueberry, Cantaloupe, Salmon, Shell, and Watermelon
¼ yd (23 cm) each Woven Stripe in Aloe, Apple, Butterscotch, Chestnut, Embers, Gooseberry, Heather, Sulfur, and Plaster
¼ yd (23 cm) Creased in Black, or any small-scale black-and-white stripe

Backing:
3 yards (2.75 m) Zig Zag Moody, or any printed fabric with a stripey theme

Binding:
½ yd (46 cm) Woven Stripe Blueberry

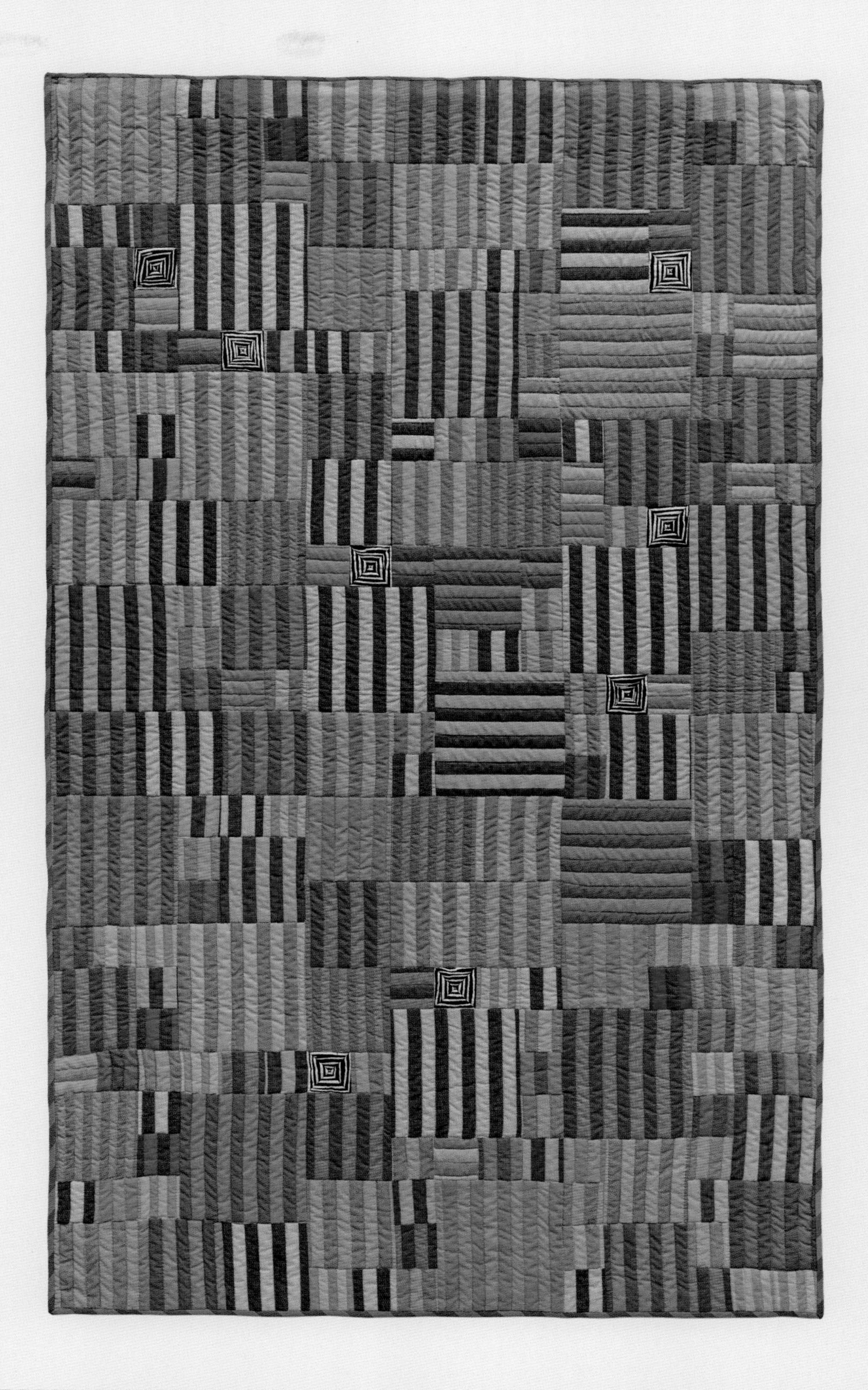

CUTTING

From Creased, or a black-and-white striped fabric, cut a strip 1⅞ inches (5 cm) wide so that the stripes run parallel to the long edges. Using a 45-degree angle, flip the ruler back and forth, cutting the strip into triangles. Make 32 triangles.

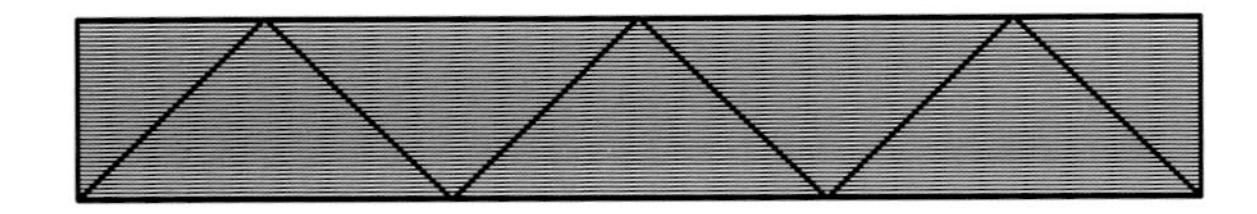

From the remaining fabric, cut an assortment of Woven Stripes.
Large squares are cut 8 × 8 inches (20 × 20 cm).
Make 20 squares.
Medium squares are cut 5½ × 5½ inches (14 × 14 cm).
Make 52 squares.
Small squares are cut 3 × 3 inches (7.5 × 7.5 cm).
Make 126 squares.

For the backing:

Cut the backing fabric in half so that there are two panels measuring approximately 54 × 40 inches (137 × 102 cm). Remove the selvages and sew together, making a backing that measures approximately 53 × 80 inches (134.6 × 220 cm).

For the binding:

Cut the stripe 2½ inches (6 cm) wide on the bias. Make at least 240 inches (6.25 m) of bias binding. Fold in half, wrong sides together, and press.

ASSEMBLING

At first glance, it may look like piecing this quilt could be a challenge, but it is quite easy. There are no set-in seams! With the help of a design wall, just follow the diagram and place the three sizes of squares together as shown. Then sew them together into three long columns.

Assembling the 8 mitered small blocks:

To make the small black-and-white blocks, choose 4 triangles and sew them together, as in the diagram on page 133.
Do not try to match up the stripes. Press. Make 8 blocks.

Assembling the top:

It is best to place patches on a design wall, following the diagram. Most stripes are to be placed so that the stripe runs vertically. Occasional placement of stripes running horizontally adds interest.
Being careful not to place the same fabrics next to each other, arrange the fabrics in three columns, as in the diagram.
Assemble each column, following the diagram, then sew the three columns together.

FINISHING

Layer the top, batting, and backing. Baste. With a deep, neutral thread, quilt along some of the stripes.
Trim. Bind.

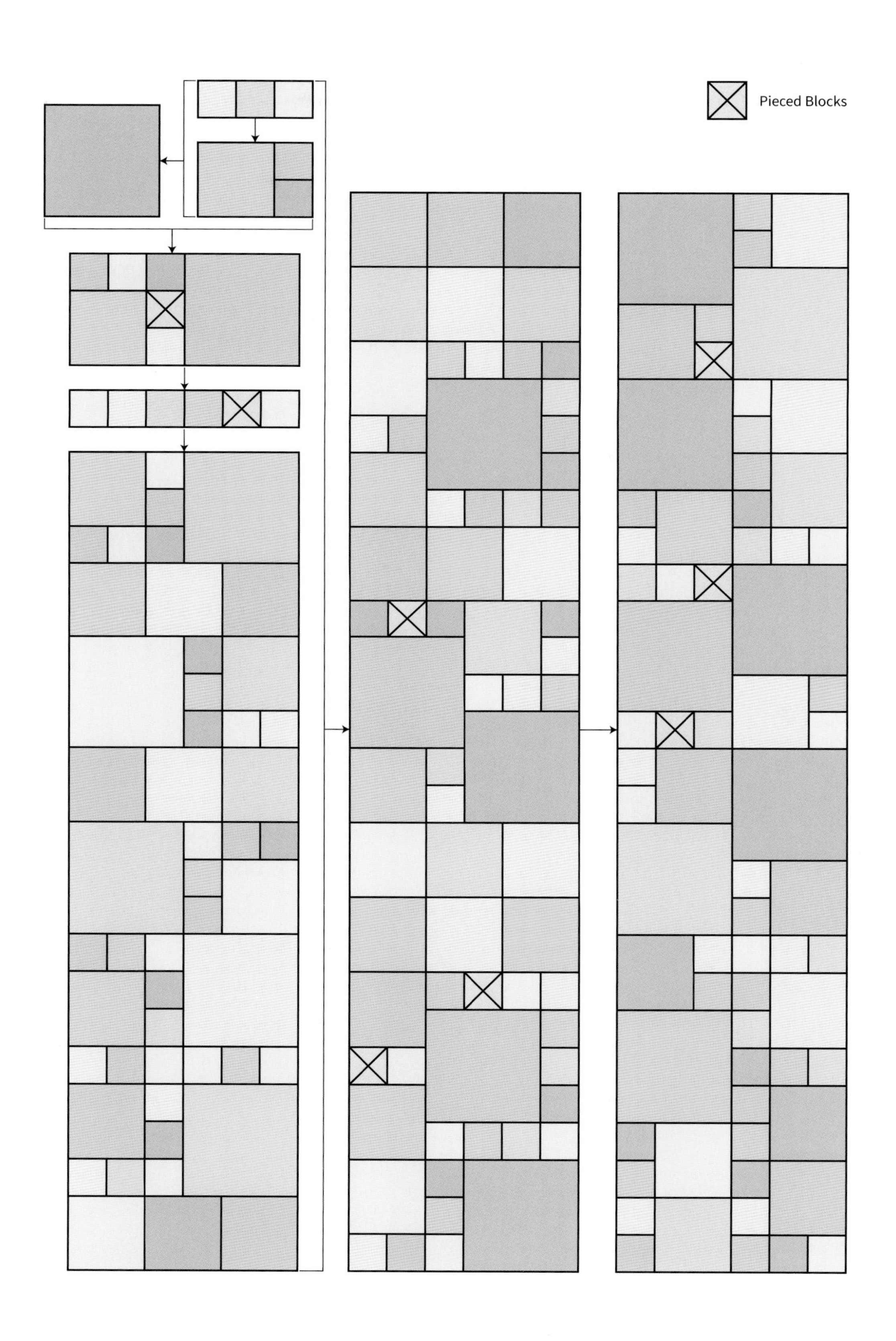
Pieced Blocks

DIAGONAL BRICKS

What I wanted to achieve with this arrangement was a landscape of texture where each print almost merged with its neighbor. I threw in a couple of highlights that underline the structure, namely the Pencils in high autumn colors and the Cocoa Onion Rings. The oblong shape of each "brick" is the perfect shape for the organic stripes in the prints. I kept the palette as close to nature as possible, with the addition of bright pink to heighten the mix and keep it from becoming just a brown sludge of a piece.

You could use any stripes that are irregular and try to find organic, marble-like structures to make a rich combination. Keeping the palette to one color mood is good, but be sure to include some heightened color tones. You could add a border or two to enlarge this idea, or just add more layers of bricks. The whole composition should hold together as a harmonious whole, so most of the prints should be the same level of color with a few darker and lighter than the majority.

FINISHED SIZE

57 × 66½ inches
(144.5 × 169 cm)

FABRIC CHOICES

The fabrics shown here are all from the Kaffe Fassett Collective—Agate, Zig Zag, Tree Fungi, Onion Rings, and Jupiter.

½ yard (46 cm) Fabric A
¼ yard (23 cm) Fabric B
¾ yard (68.5 cm) Fabric C
½ yard (46 cm) Fabric D
½ yard (46 cm) Fabric E
½ yard (46 cm) Fabric F
½ yard (46 cm) Fabric G
½ yard (46 cm) Fabric H
½ yard (46 cm) Fabric I
¼ yard (23 cm) Fabric J
¼ yard (23 cm) Fabric K

Backing:
3¾ yards (3.5 m)

Binding:
½ yard (46 cm)

CUTTING

The full-size bricks are cut 4 × 10 inches (10 × 25 cm).
The half-size bricks are cut 4 × 5¼ inches (10 × 13 cm).
Note: Fabrics A and C are used twice.
Before cutting, pay attention to the direction of the stripes or striations in the fabrics chosen. The stripes and striations should run horizontally in the bricks.
Fabric A—Cut 8 full size. Cut 4 half size.
Fabric B—Cut 5 full size. Cut 1 half size.
Fabric C—Cut 16 full size. Cut 2 half size.
Fabric D—Cut 9 full size. Cut 1 half size.
Fabric E—Cut 11 full size. Cut 1 half size.
Fabric F—Cut 11 full size. Cut 2 half size.
Fabric G—Cut 11 full size. Cut 2 half size.
Fabric H—Cut 11 full size. Cut 2 half size.
Fabric I—Cut 11 full size. Cut 1 half size.
Fabric J—Cut 7 full size. Cut 1 half size.
Fabric K—Cut 5 full size. Cut 1 half size.

For the backing:

Cut 2 lengths measuring approximately 40 × 65 inches (102 × 165 cm). Remove selvages. Sew together, making a backing that measures approximately 80 × 65 inches (2 m × 165 cm). Trim to approximately 75 × 65 inches (190.5 × 165 cm).

For the binding:

Cut 7 strips 2½ inches (6 cm) wide from selvage to selvage. Remove selvages.
Sew end to end.

ASSEMBLING

Using the diagram to guide color placement, sew the bricks into 19 horizontal rows. Sew the rows together.

FINISHING

Press. Layer top, batting, and backing. Baste. Quilt using rust colored thread in horizontal, wavy lines throughout.
Trim. Bind.

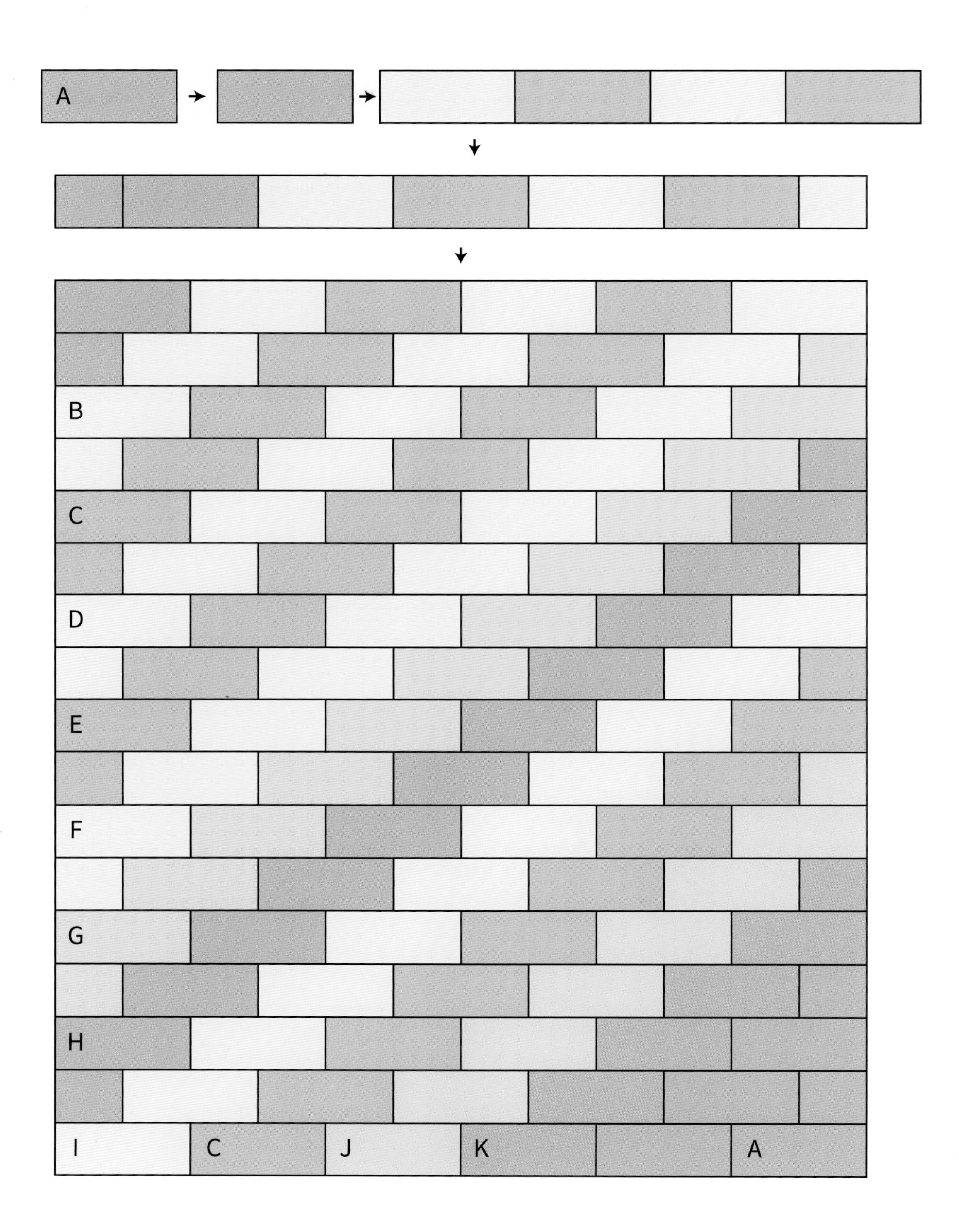
A
B
C
D
E
F
G
H
I
C
J
K
A

OPTICAL STRIPES

Brandon's prints make this quilt. The sashing is done in his Zig Zag print and, best of all, the background of each block is his black-and-white Sharks Teeth. I was trying to almost lose my squares of striped prints in the black and white Sharks Teeth base.

Once I had this textural base established, I chose stripey prints that were pastel in tone and in a level of color that almost merged with the Sharks Teeth base. It was fun finding all the different complex stripes. Some were striped fans, zig zags, ribbons, and striped paisleys. Many of the prints are neutral in coloring, so they fade into the black-and-white base of each block, but there are enough high colors that sing out and keep the quilt lively to behold.

You could use any two-color textural print to replace the Sharks Teeth, but a strong contrast is needed. Then find prints that sing, or melt, into your background. Be careful to have them be all the same level of tone—all dark or medium or light—so the eye travels easily over the whole composition. This idea could be done all in spots and dots as well.

FINISHED SIZE

71 × 82½ inches
(1.8 × 2.1 m)

FABRIC CHOICES

Fabrics featured in the squares are all from the Kaffe Fassett Collective and were selected for their graphic designs in a chalky pastel palette. Some of these have been stashed away for years. The Sharks Teeth border fabric and the Zig Zag sashing are currently available.

- Scraps to ¼ yard (23 cm) each of at least 15 different chalky pastel fabrics
- 2¾ yards (2.5 m) Sharks Teeth Black
- 2 yards (183 cm) Zig Zag White
- ½ yard (46 cm) Onion Rings Black

Backing:

2½ yards (228.5 cm) 108-inch (2.7 m) wide Onion Ring Black

Binding:

¾ yard (68.5 cm) Spot Periwinkle

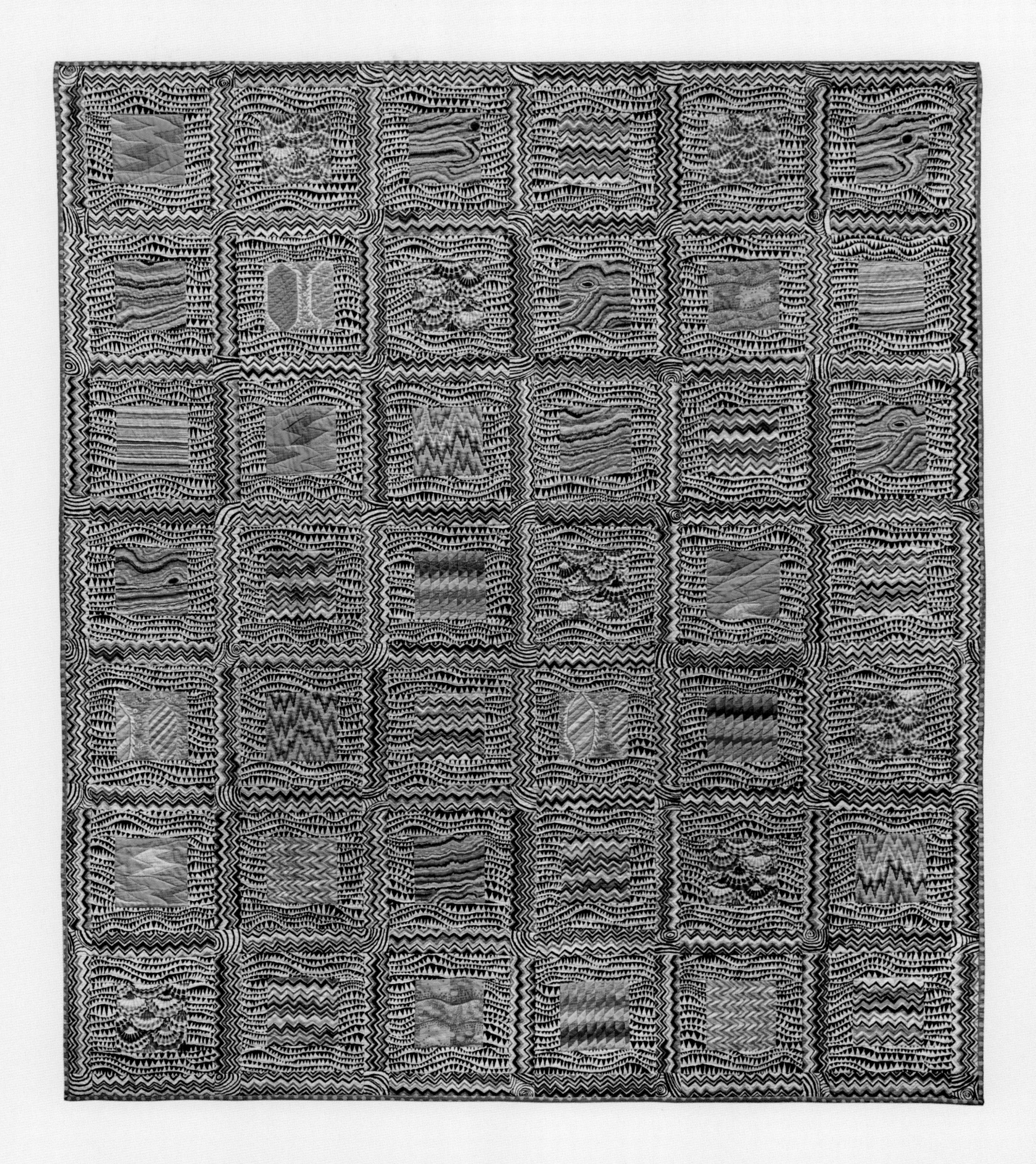

CUTTING

From an assortment of chalky pastel fabrics, cut 42 squares measuring 6 × 6 inches (15 × 15 cm).
Important: Pay attention to the direction of the Sharks Teeth and Zig Zag before cutting.

From Sharks Teeth:

Cut 6 strips measuring 6 inches (15 cm), selvage to selvage. Crosscut at 2½ inches (6 cm). Each strip will yield 16 rectangles measuring 2½ × 6 inches (6 × 15 cm). Cut a total of 84 rectangles.
Cut 21 strips measuring 2½ inches (6 cm), selvage to selvage. Crosscut at 10 inches (25 cm). Each strip will yield 4 rectangles measuring 2½ × 10 inches (6 × 25 cm).
Cut a total of 84 rectangles.

From Zig Zag:

Cut 25 strips measuring 2½ inches (6 cm) wide, selvage to selvage. Crosscut at 10 inches (25 cm). Each strip will yield 4 rectangles measuring 2½ × 10 inches (6 × 25 cm). Cut a total of 97 rectangles.

From Onion Rings:

Cut 56 squares measuring 2½ × 2½ inches (6 × 6 cm) for the corner stones.

For the backing:

Prepare a backing that measures approximately 80 × 91 inches (2 × 2.3 m).

For the binding:

Cut 8 strips measuring 2½ inches (6 cm) wide, selvage to selvage. Remove the selvages.
Sew end to end.

ASSEMBLING

If the fabrics chosen for the center squares are directional, pay attention to the direction and place them upright before sewing the Sharks Teeth to the squares.
For each block, sew the two shorter Sharks Teeth rectangles to the sides. Sew the longer two rectangles to the top and bottom. Make 42 blocks.
Alternate 7 Zig Zag sashing rectangles and 6 blocks for each row. Make 7 rows.
Alternate 7 Onion Ring cornerstones with 6 Zig Zag sashing rectangles and make 8 horizontal sashing strips.
Alternate the horizontal sashing strips and the block rows and sew together.

FINISHING

Press. Layer top, batting, and backing. Baste. Quilt using white thread around the details in the colored blocks. Quilt zigzagging lines in the block borders and sashing.
Trim. Bind.

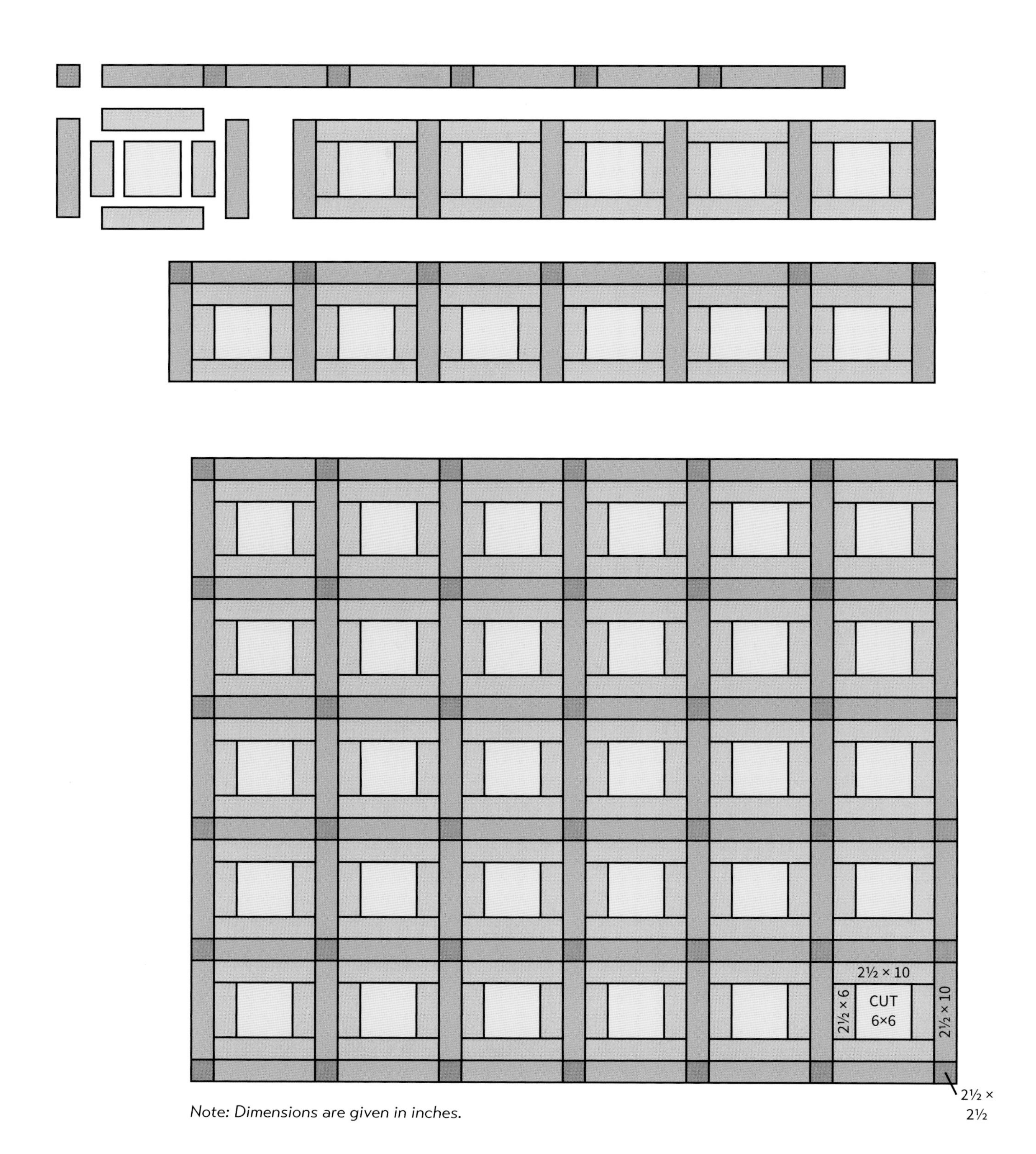

Note: Dimensions are given in inches.

BLUE SUZANI

It's important to keep colors in this work in close harmony. You could add more contrast with shades of red on white, or with a gray base and pastel tones. I hand-quilted the central circles, doing a curlicue at the center of each circle. The rest of the piece was machine quilted.

FINISHED SIZE

72 × 72 inches (183 × 183 cm)

FABRIC CHOICES

- 1¼ yards (114 cm) each Regal Fans Blue and Regal Fans Dark
- 2½ yards (2.3 m) Woven Stripe Mallard (includes binding)
- 1 yard (91 cm) each Shot Cotton Teal, Heliotrope, Lupin, Emerald, Pistachio, and Aubergine
- ½ yard (46 cm) Shot Cotton Glacier
- 1 yard (91 cm) Woven Stripe Embers

Backing:

4¾ yards (4.3 m)

NOTIONS

- Aurifil 12 wt cotton thread in brightly colored blues, pinks, and greens
- Fabric glue stick
- Straight pins
- Freezer paper, or large cardboard, to make circle templates

CUTTING

For the center background:

Cut 18 squares measuring 8½ × 8½ inches (21.5 × 21.5 cm) each from Regal Fans Blue and Regal Fans Dark

Suggestion: Spray the Shot Cotton with Mary Ellen's Best Press or fabric sizing before cutting.

Using paper or freezer paper, make one template each for circles that are 18 inches (46 cm) in diameter, 10½ inches (26.5 cm) in diameter, 5½ inches (14 cm) in diameter, and 4 inches (10 cm) in diameter.

Cut the large circles first. Using the templates, draw circles on the fabric and cut with fabric scissors, keeping the fabric as stiff as possible.

Cut one 18-inch (46 cm) diameter circle from each Shot Cotton—Teal, Pistachio, Lupin, Emerald

Cut one 10½-inch (26.5 cm) diameter circle from Shot Cotton Heliotrope

Cut one 5½-inch (14 cm) diameter circle from each Shot Cotton Pistachio, Emerald

Cut two 5½-inch (14 cm) diameter circles from Shot Cotton Lupin

Cut two 4-inch (10 cm) diameter circles from Shot Cotton Teal

Cut one 4-inch (10 cm) diameter circle from each Shot Cotton Pistachio, Emerald

For the Snowballs:

Cut all squares to 4½ × 4½ inches (11.5 × 11.5 cm). Cut 18–19 squares each from Shot Cotton Teal, Heliotrope, Pistachio, Lupin, Glacier, and Emerald, for a total of 112 squares.

For the Snowball corners:

Cut 18 strips from Shot Cotton Aubergine measuring 1½ inches (4 cm) wide, selvage to selvage. Crosscut at 1½ inches (4 cm), making 26 squares from each strip. A total of 448 squares are needed.

For the border:

Using Woven Stripe Embers, cut 7 strips measuring 4½ inches (11.5 cm) wide from selvage to selvage. Remove selvages. Sew end to end. Cut 4 lengths measuring 64½ inches (164 cm) Cut 4 corner stone blocks measuring 4½ × 4½ inches (11.5 × 11.5 cm), cutting 2 from Regal Fans Blue and 2 from Regal Fans Dark.

For the circle edgings:

Using Woven Stripe Mallard, cut a 40-inch (102 cm) length from the stripe. Cut that yardage 1 inch (2.5 cm) wide into a continuous bias strip. Fold the strip wrong sides together and press, making about 12 yards (11 m) of 1-inch (2.5 cm) wide bias edging.

For the binding:

With the remaining stripe yardage, cut a continuous bias strip measuring 2½ inches (6 cm) wide, making it at least 296 inches (7.5 m) long.

For the backing:

Cut 2 lengths measuring approximately 80 inches (2 m) long. Remove selvages. Sew together to make a backing that measures approximately 80 × 80 inches (2 × 2 m).

ASSEMBLING

Center:

Sew the background: Alternating the two colors of Regal Palm, sew 6 squares into a row. Press the seams open. Sew 6 rows. Sew the rows together. Press the seams open.

Following the diagram for placement, arrange the circles on the quilt, center, and pin in place. Glue baste each circle and remove the pins. Starting with the big circles, working one at a time, pin the bias edges around each circle, aligning the raw edges of the binding with the raw edges of the circle. Where the ends meet, fold in the end of one end and tuck it into the other end. Machine stitch the edging in place ¼ inch (.5 cm) from the raw edges.

Do this for each circle. For the smaller circles, be extra generous with the bias edging, making tiny pleats as you go so that it will fall flat while you turn it back. Press the bias edges away from the circles. Using a dark blue thread, topstitch the edges down, staying very close to the folded edge.

Assembling the Snowball border:

Make Snowballs. For each Snowball, choose one 4½-inch (11.5 cm) square and four 1½-inch (4 cm) Aubergine squares. Make 112 Snowballs following this diagram.

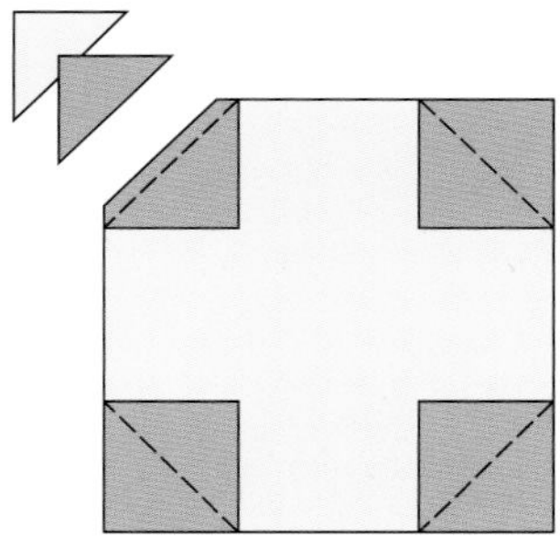

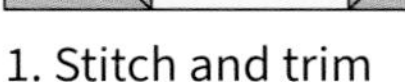

1. Stitch and trim

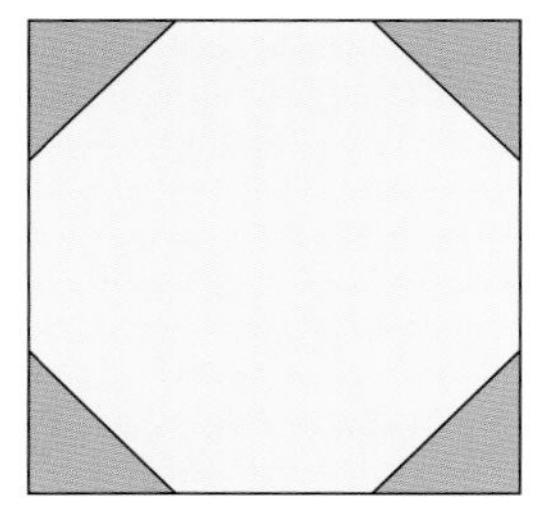

2. Press open

Arrange the Snowballs randomly so that there is a good color mix.

Sew 24 Snowballs together as in the diagram for the top and bottom borders.

Sew 32 Snowballs together as in the diagram for the side borders.

Sew the top and bottom borders to the center.

Sew two striped borders to the sides. Sew Royal Fans squares to each end of the remaining two stripe borders and sew to the top and bottom.

FINISHING

Press. Layer top, batting, and backing. Baste. Machine quilt using blue thread throughout the background and make swirls in the Snowballs. The circles are hand-quilted with the Aurifil 12 wt thread, making big stitches in concentric circles. Use a thread that contrasts with the color of the circle.

Trim. Bind.

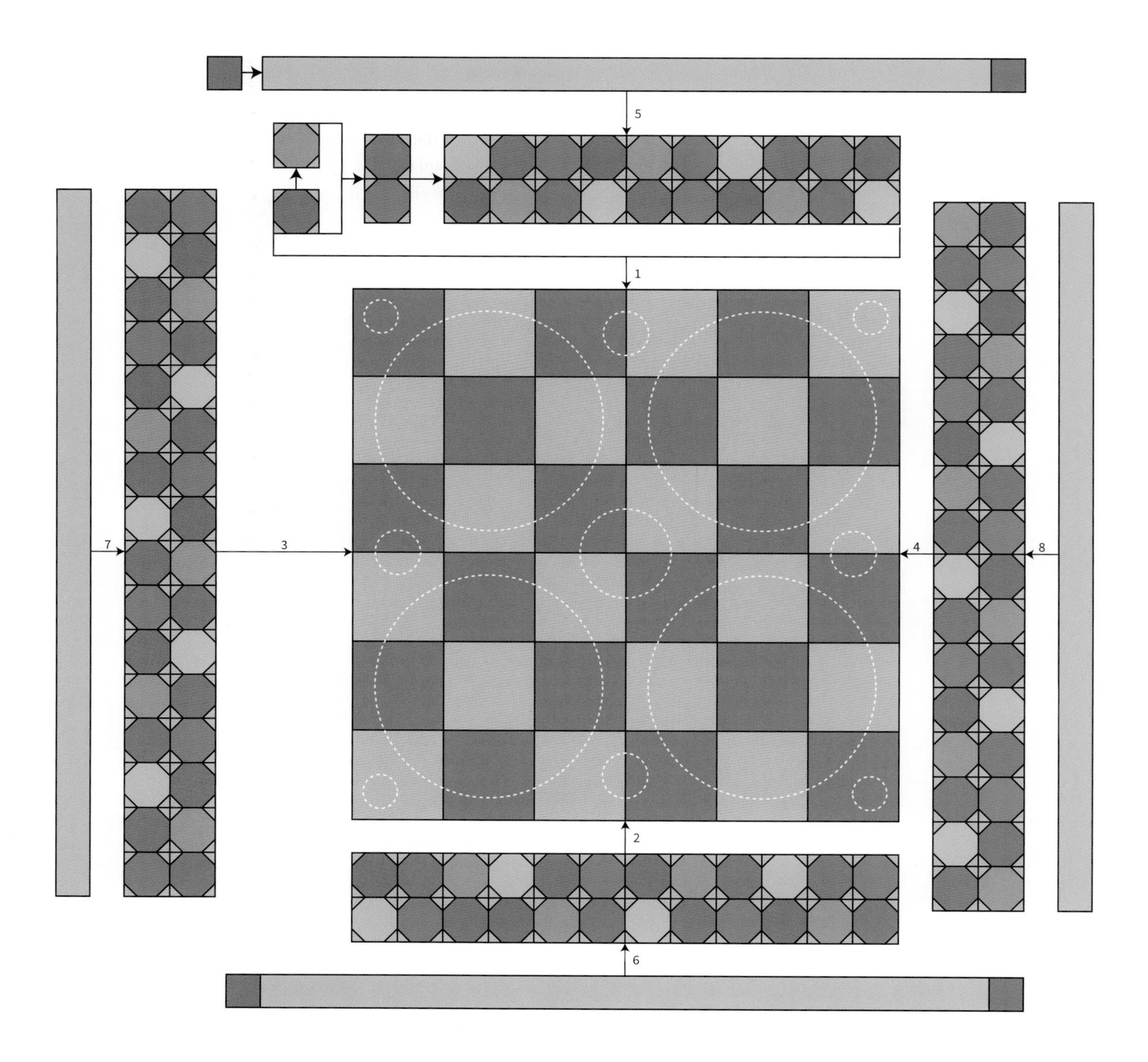

CIRCLE LOG CABIN

The main idea of this quilt is to find different scales of bold circular prints. The eye wants to be excited to discover huge circles next to medium and small, precise circles in your prints. I've included my Rainbow half-circle print as well as overlapping round Poppies, but the prints that really tell your story are the articulate circles in rows.

Circles can be round florals or fruit prints like my Oranges, and many geometric designs can be found in your local quilt shop. Some of the patches with distinct borders, like the Oranges, are fussy cut to make this a carefully composed quilt.

You can see I've kept this layout in high pastels, but you can see from other quilts in this book that darker, more luminous palettes give a rich effect too. My advice is not to vary the level of color too much. Find enough prints in your chosen palette that are similar in tone but not so "samey" that they mush together. Throw in some surprising elements to keep the arrangement alive.

FINISHED SIZE

68 × 72 inches (173 × 183 cm)

FABRIC CHOICES

Because so many of the fabrics are fussy cut, the amounts given for each round below are only estimates. When in doubt, get more yardage for each round. Some of the fabrics we used are Oranges in Pink, Damask Flower in Lilac, and Rainbows in White.

Center:

1 scrap at least 9 × 13 inches (23 × 33 cm)
Round 1: ½ yard (46 cm)
Round 2: ¼ yard (23 cm)
Round 3: ½ yard (46 cm)
Round 4: ½ yard (46 cm)
Round 5: ⅜ yard (34 cm)
Round 6: ¼ yard (23 cm)
Round 7: ¾ yard (68.5 cm)
Round 8: ½ yard (46 cm)
Round 9: 1¼ yards (114 cm)
Round 10: ¾ yard (68.5 cm)
Round 11: ¾ yard (68.5 cm)

Backing:

4½ yards (4 m) of a circular or dotty print

Binding:

¾ yard (68.5 cm) Spots Mauve

CUTTING

Keep in mind that, if fussy cutting, you must pay attention to the print as you cut these pieces. When the length cut is more than 46 inches (117 cm), it will be necessary to seam two pieces together to get the right length.

Center: Cut one piece measuring 8½ × 12½ inches (21.5 × 32 cm).
Round 1: Cut two pieces measuring 4½ × 12½ inches (11.5 × 32 cm) and two measuring 4½ × 16½ inches (11.5 × 42 cm).
Round 2: Cut two pieces measuring 2 × 20½ inches (5 × 52 cm) and two measuring 2 × 19½ inches (5 × 49.5 cm).
Round 3: Cut two pieces measuring 3 × 23½ inches (7.5 × 59.5 cm) and two measuring 3 × 24½ inches (7.5 × 62 cm).
Round 4: Cut two pieces measuring 4 × 28½ inches (10 × 72 cm) and two measuring 4 × 31½ inches (10 × 80 cm).
Round 5: Cut two pieces measuring 2 × 35½ inches (5 × 90 cm) and two measuring 2 × 34½ inches (5 × 87.5 cm).
Round 6: Cut two pieces measuring 1 × 38½ inches (2.5 × 98 cm) and two measuring 1 × 35½ inches (2.5 × 90 cm).
Round 7: Cut two pieces measuring 4½ × 39½ inches (11.5 × 100 cm) and two measuring 4½ × 43½ inches (11.5 × 110.5 cm).
Round 8: Cut two pieces measuring 2½ × 47½ inches (6 × 120.5 cm) and two measuring 2½ × 47½ inches (6 × 120.5 cm).
Round 9: Cut two pieces measuring 6½ × 51½ inches (16.5 × 131 cm) and two measuring 6½ × 59½ inches (16.5 × 151 cm).
Round 10: Cut two pieces measuring 2½ × 63½ inches (6 × 161 cm) and two measuring 2½ × 63½ inches (6 × 161 cm).
Round 11: Cut two pieces measuring 3 × 67½ inches (7.5 × 171.5 cm) and two measuring 3 × 68½ inches (7.5 × 174 cm).

Backing:

Cut into 2 pieces measuring approximately 40 × 80 inches (102 cm × 2 m). Remove selvages and sew together, making a backing approximately 80 × 80 inches (2 × 2 m).

Binding:

Cut 6 strips from selvage to selvage. Remove selvages. Sew end to end.

ASSEMBLING

The quilt is worked from the center out.
Round 1: Sew the shorter lengths to the sides of the center. Sew the longer lengths to the top and bottom.
Continue in this manner, sewing sides first then top and bottom for each round.

FINISHING

Press. Layer top, batting, and backing. Quilt as desired.

Trim. Bind.

Note: the dimensions represent the cutting measurements, not finished size.

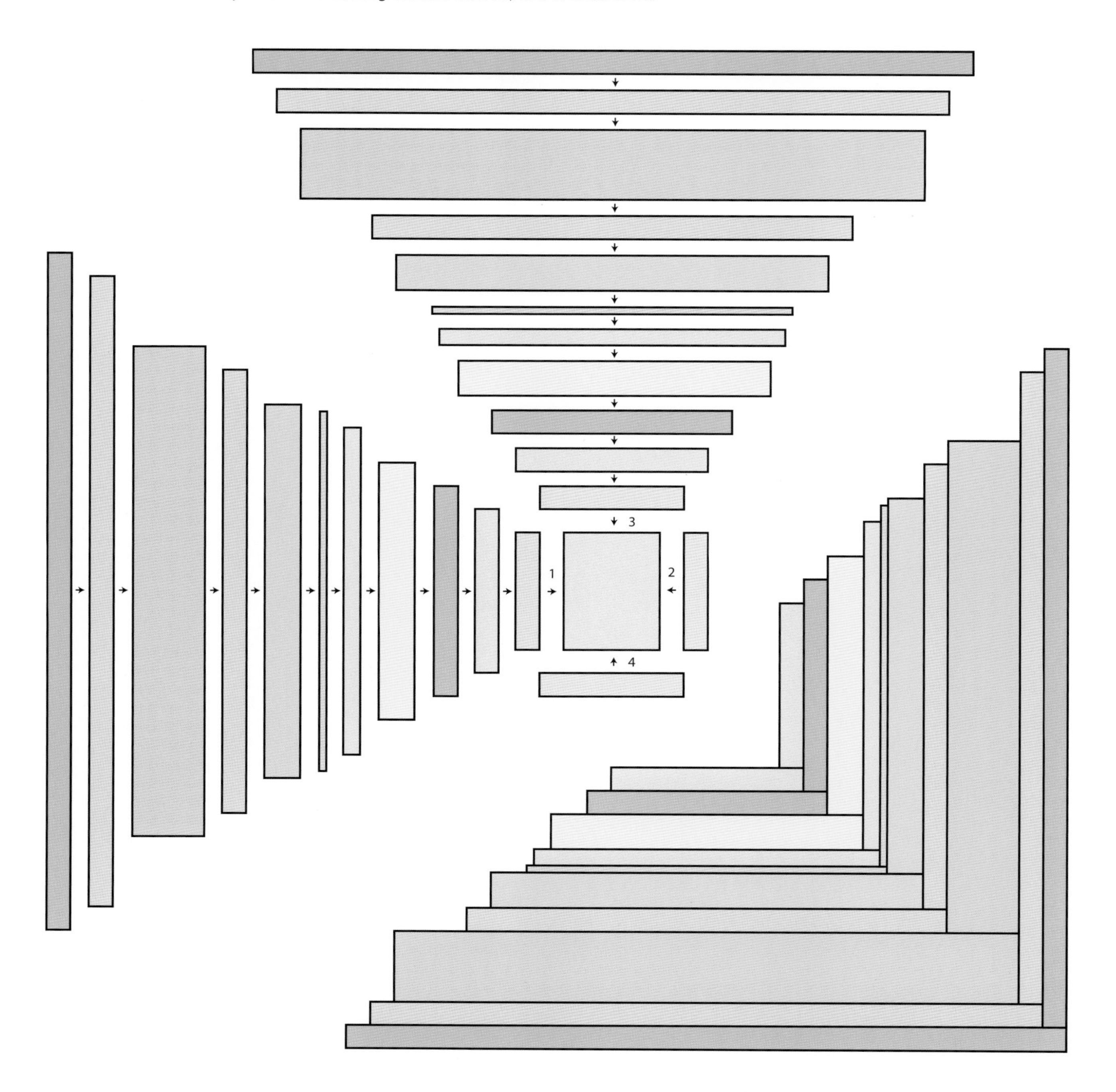

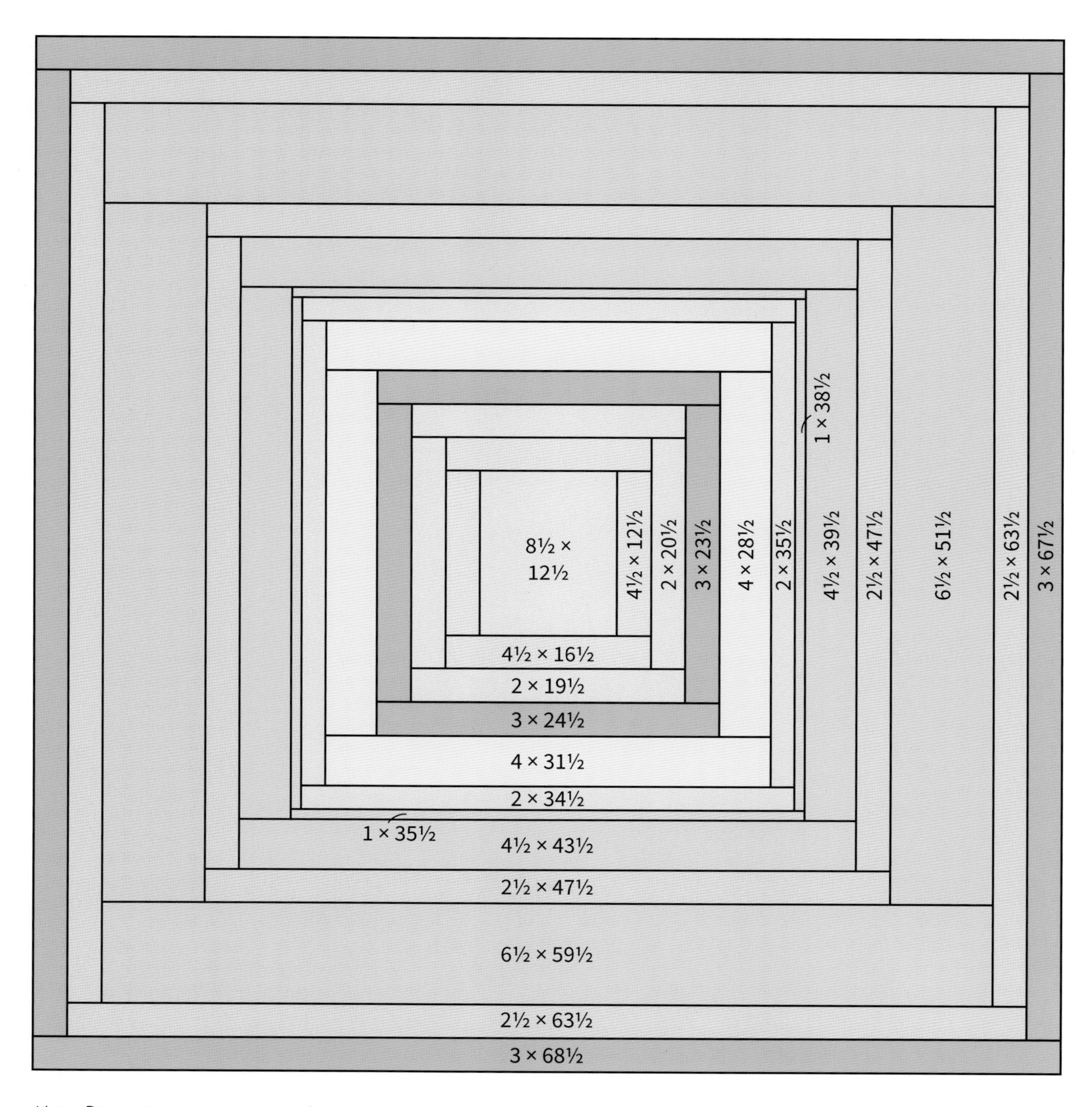

Note: Dimensions are given in inches.

SUNRISE

This is actually a one-patch quilt, which means that the entire quilt is made from only one-size patch. It is based on a traditional Lone Star pattern, except with Sunrise, the patches go all the way to the edges of the quilt, making it look less like a twinkling star and more like an exploding one!

To get the colors right, be sure each diamond merges a little with its neighbors, but still holds its own with an occasional dramatic contrast, such as the blue print meeting the orange and yellow on the fourth and fifth rows. It's surprising how a larger print works in these small diamonds. If the print is too small, it just becomes a flat texture and stops the fizz that the more pronounced prints create.

There are "quick" strip-piecing methods to make Lone Star quilts, but to make a good and harmonious sequence of color, there is no short cut for placing individual diamonds on a design wall. It isn't necessary to arrange the whole quilt; just place diamonds for one wedge starting with the center and fanning out.

FINISHED SIZE

95 inches × 95 inches (2.4 m × 2.4 m).

FABRIC CHOICES

This quilt has eight sections. It makes figuring out how much fabric you will need easy because you can get 8 diamonds from a 2¾-inch (7 cm) selvage-to-selvage strip. As the star grows, it grows in multiples of eight. For example, the center, which is row 1, has 8 diamonds, row 2 has 16, row 3 has 24 and so on. Until you get to row 15, which has 120 diamonds, this formula will work. After row 15 the number of diamonds will change, as rows 16–21 are only needed to fill in the corners.

Row 1: (center) ⅛ yard (11.5 cm)
Row 2: ¼ yard (23 cm)
Row 3: ⅜ yard (34 cm)
Row 4: ½ yard (46 cm)
Row 5: ½ yard (46 cm)
Row 6: ⅝ yard (57 cm)
Row 7: ⅝ yard (57 cm)
Row 8: ¾ yard (68.5 cm)
Row 9: ⅞ yard (80 cm)
Row 10: ⅞ yard (80 cm)
Row 11: 1 yard (91 cm)
Row 12: 1⅛ yards (103 cm)
Row 13: 1⅛ yards (103 cm)
Row 14: 1¼ yards (114 cm)
Row 15: 1⅜ yards (126 cm)
Row 16: 1⅜ yards (126 cm)
Row 17: 1⅛ yards (103 cm)
Row 18: ⅞ yard (80 cm)
Row 19: ¾ yard (68.5 cm)
Row 20: ½ yard (46 cm)
Row 21: ⅜ yard (34 cm)

Backing:

3 yards (2.7 m) of 108-inch (2.7 m) wide backing fabric

Binding:

1 yard (91 cm)

CUTTING

Cutting Tip:

Here is a tip for cutting and sewing that can help with sewing all the bias edges together. Eight diamonds are cut 2¾ inches (7 cm) wide from one strip cut selvage to selvage. If you fold the fabric in half when cutting the diamonds, 4 diamonds will have bias edges on two sides and the other 4 diamonds will have bias edges on the opposite two sides. If you keep them in separate piles and are very organized as you go, you can sew the diamonds together with a bias edge matched against a straight grain edge.

Cut the required number of 2¾-inch (7 cm) wide strips, selvage to selvage. Then, using Template A, cut 8 diamonds from each strip or, using a ruler with diagonal markings, lop off the end at a 45-degree angle, move the ruler over 2¾ inches (7 cm), and cut. Continue in this manner for 8 diamonds from each strip. Cut the following number of strips and diamonds.

Row	Strips	Diamonds
1	1	8
2	2	16
3	3	24
4	4	32
5	5	40
6	6	48
7	7	56
8	8	64
9	9	72
10	10	80
11	11	88
12	12	96
13	13	104
14	14	112
15	15	120
16	15	120
17	13	104
18	10	80
19	8	64
20	5	40
21	3	24

Backing:

Trim the 108-inch (2.7 m) backing to approximately 104 × 104 inches (2.6 × 2.6 m)

Binding:

Cut 10 strips measuring 2½ inches (6.5 cm) wide from selvage to selvage.
Remove selvages. Sew end to end.

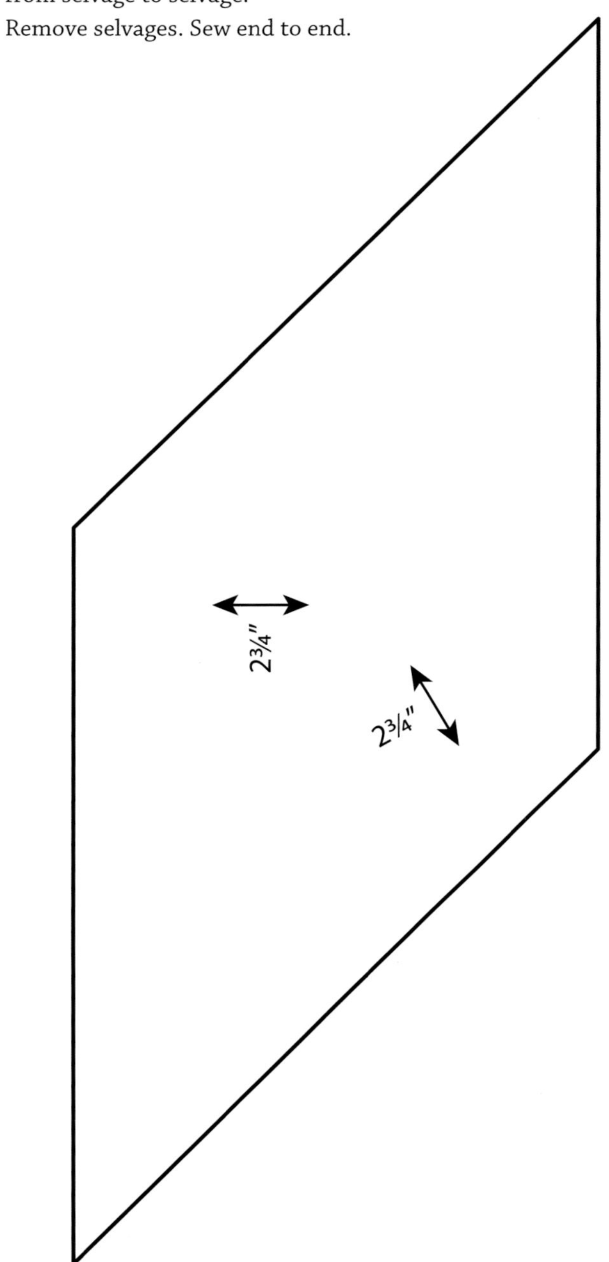

ASSEMBLING

Follow the diagram to sew diamonds into long strips to make 8 full wedges. NOTE! Pay attention to the angle!
For 4 of the pieced star wedges, the diamonds are sewn together thus:

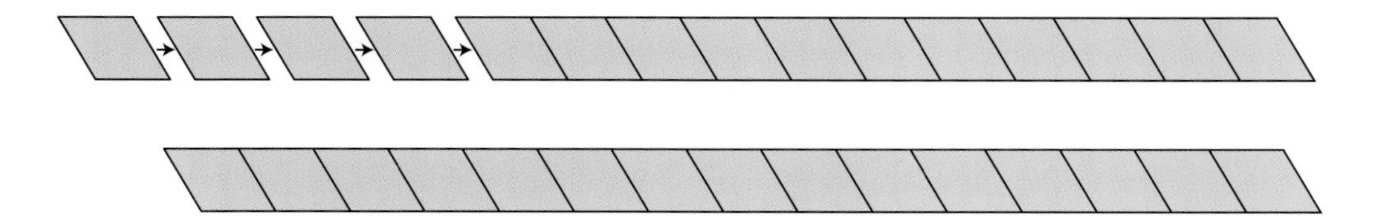

For the other 4, the diamonds are sewn together thus:

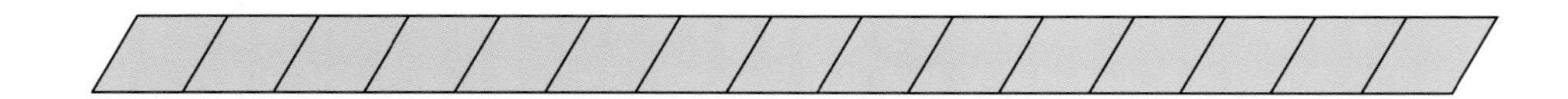

When all the diamonds are sewn into strips, sew the strips together.

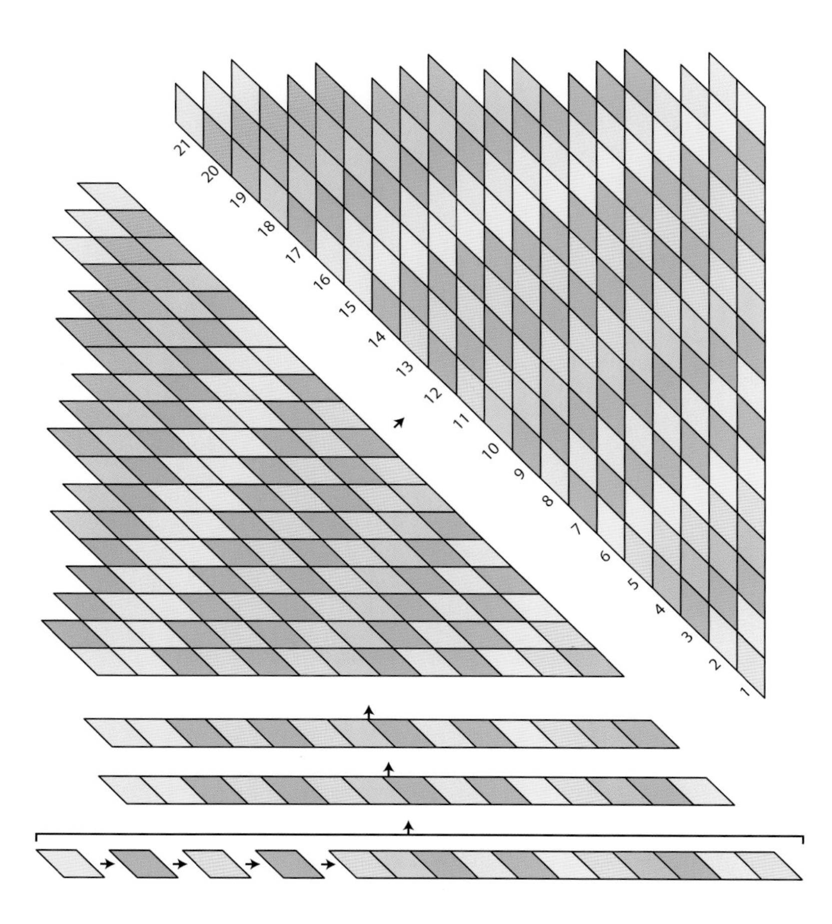

Make 8 star wedges. Sew 2 wedges together to make a quarter of the top and press the center seam open. Do this four times. Sew these quarters together, pressing the seam open as you go. This way the center 8 diamonds will come together easily.
Press flat. Use a washable marker, pencil, or painter's tape to mark the line where the corners will be squared off. Cut off the excess about 1 inch (2.5 cm) beyond the mark.

FINISHING

Layer top, batting, and backing. Baste. Quilt using a thread that harmonizes with the colors you have used, meandering throughout.
Trim off at the marked edges. Bind.

FLOWERY VASES

The first thing I did for this quilt was to create a blue base for my vases so the floors and background to each block had a deep, cool feeling. This helped me find good contrasting florals on a large scale to make my vases come alive. Each print had a blue, green, or purple element in it that harmonized with my backgrounds. There is enough contrast in the florals to bring the vase to life without being so contrasting that it stops the eye from moving over the whole composition. The mirror imaging is vital here, and it gives a good balance to the whole quilt. Another critical element is to keep the backgrounds small-scale to contrast and highlight the vases.

FINISHED SIZE

94 × 102 inches (2.4 × 2.6 m)

FABRIC CHOICES

All the fabrics here are in the current collections. It is possible to make the vases with less yardage, but because many of the fabrics used are directional, and fussy cutting is desirable, the amount listed is ample.

Vases:

There are 5 different vase templates. Some fabrics are used more than once.

1 yard (91 cm) each of 8 vase fabrics
- Lake Blossoms Black
- Japanese Chrysanthemum Scarlet
- Shaggy Black
- Cactus Flower Cool
- Cactus Flower Tawny
- Hokusai's Mums Natural
- Van Gogh Green
- Van Gogh Blue

Background walls:

¾ yard (68.5 cm) each
- Ferns Periwinkle
- Ferns Purple
- Ferns Turquoise
- Moss Flower Blue
- Jumble Duck Egg
- Guinea Flower Black
- Guinea Flower Blue

1 yard (91 cm) Guinea Flower Cobalt (for walls and floors)

Background floors:

½ yard (46 cm) each
- Spot Peacock
- Spot Green
- Spot Sapphire
- Spot Merlot
- Spot Aqua
- Paperweight Purple

Shadows:

½ yard (46 cm) Aboriginal Dot Orchid

Border:

2¾ yards (2.5 m) Lotus Leaf Purple

Backing:

9 yards (8.2 m)

Binding:

1 yard (91 cm) Aboriginal Dot Periwinkle

Optional based on preferred appliqué method:

Template plastic
Freezer paper
Fusible web

CUTTING

Background walls:

The 28 background walls are cut to measure 12½ × 17½ inches (32 × 44 cm).

Cut 12½ inch (32 cm) wide strips from selvage to selvage. Crosscut at 17½ inches to make 2 rectangles from each strip.

Cut 4 each from:
Ferns Periwinkle
Ferns Purple
Guinea Flower Black
Guinea Flower Blue
Moss Flower Blue

Cut 3 each from:
Ferns Turquoise
Jumble Duck Egg

Cut 2 from:
Guinea Flower Cobalt

Background floors:

The 28 Background floors are cut 6½ × 12½ inches (16.5 × 32 cm).

Cut 6 from each:
Spot Merlot
Spot Peacock

Cut 4 from each:
Spot Green
Spot Sapphire

Cut 3 from each:
Paperweight Purple
Guinea Flower Cobalt

Cut 2 from:
Spot Aqua

Borders:

From Lotus Leaf Purple, cut 2 lengths measuring 5½ × 94½ inches (140 × 240 cm) for the sides. Cut 2 lengths 5½ × 92½ inches (14 × 230 cm) for the top and bottom.

The Vase and Shadow templates should be enlarged 300% percent.

Use the dotted line to line up the vase with the sewn seam on the background block.

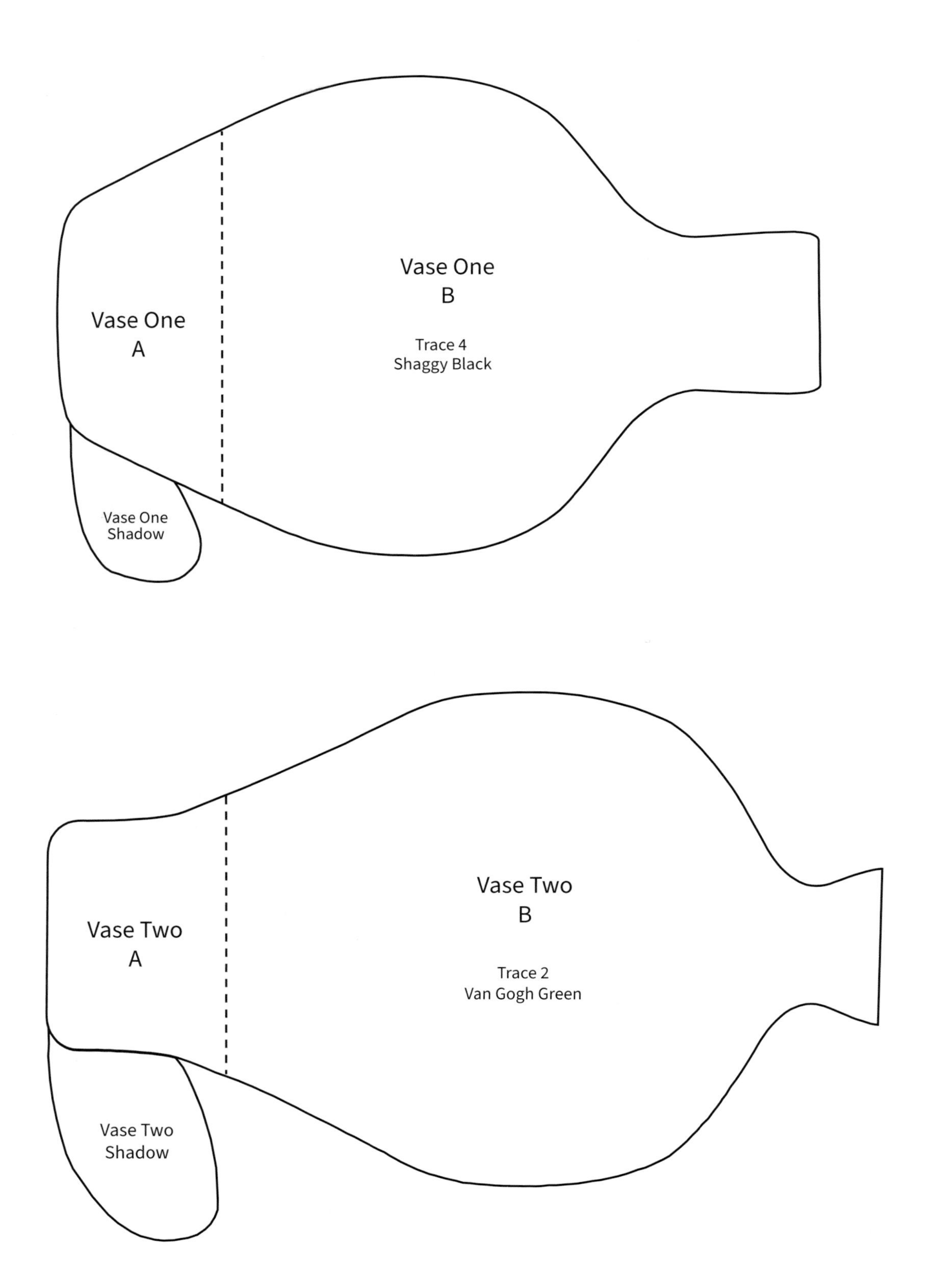
Vase One
B
Trace 4
Shaggy Black
Vase One
A
Vase One
Shadow
Vase Two
B
Trace 2
Van Gogh Green
Vase Two
A
Vase Two
Shadow

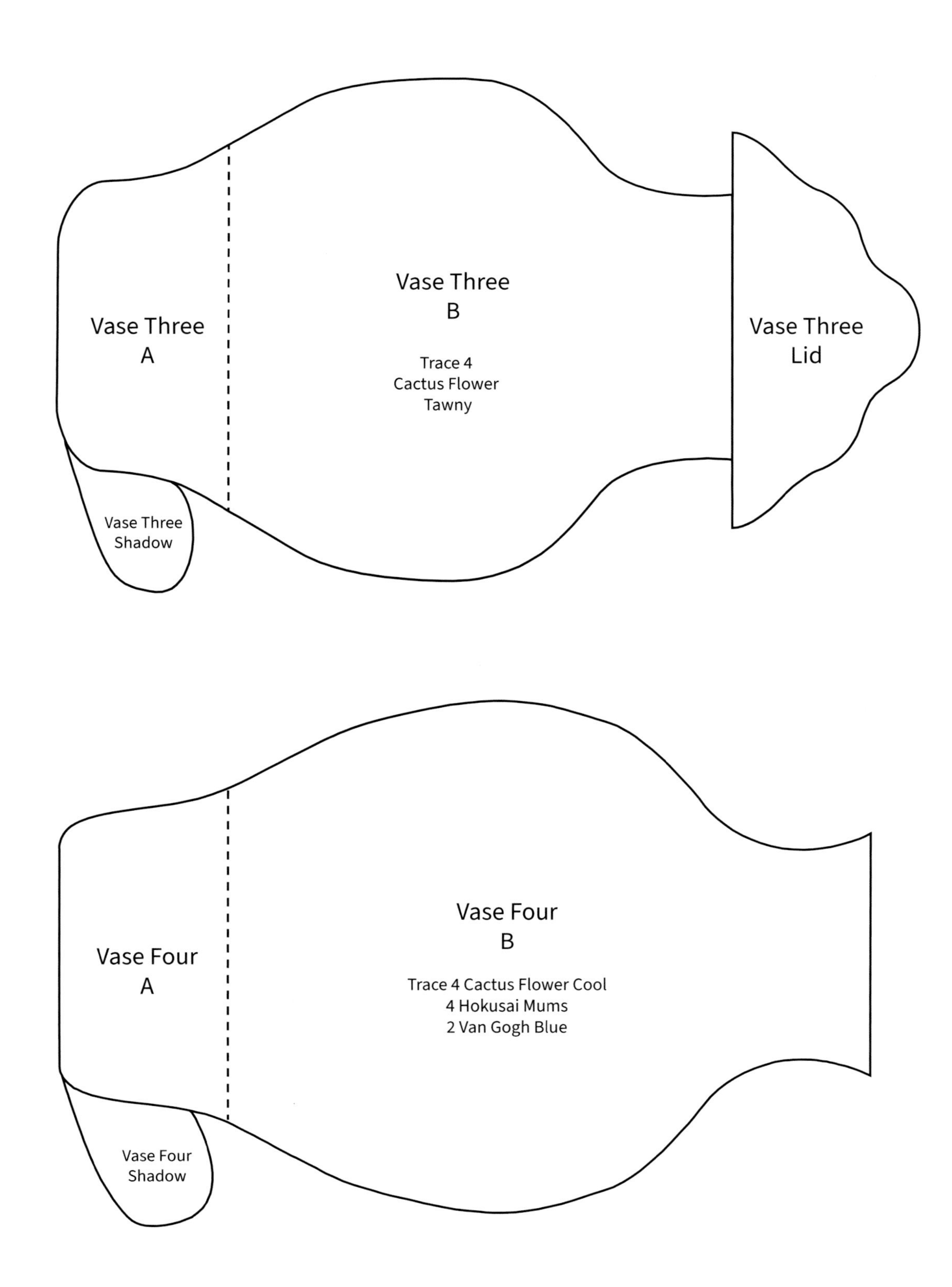
Vase Three
A
Vase Three
B
Trace 4
Cactus Flower
Tawny
Vase Three
Lid
Vase Three
Shadow
Vase Four
A
Vase Four
B
Trace 4 Cactus Flower Cool
4 Hokusai Mums
2 Van Gogh Blue
Vase Four
Shadow

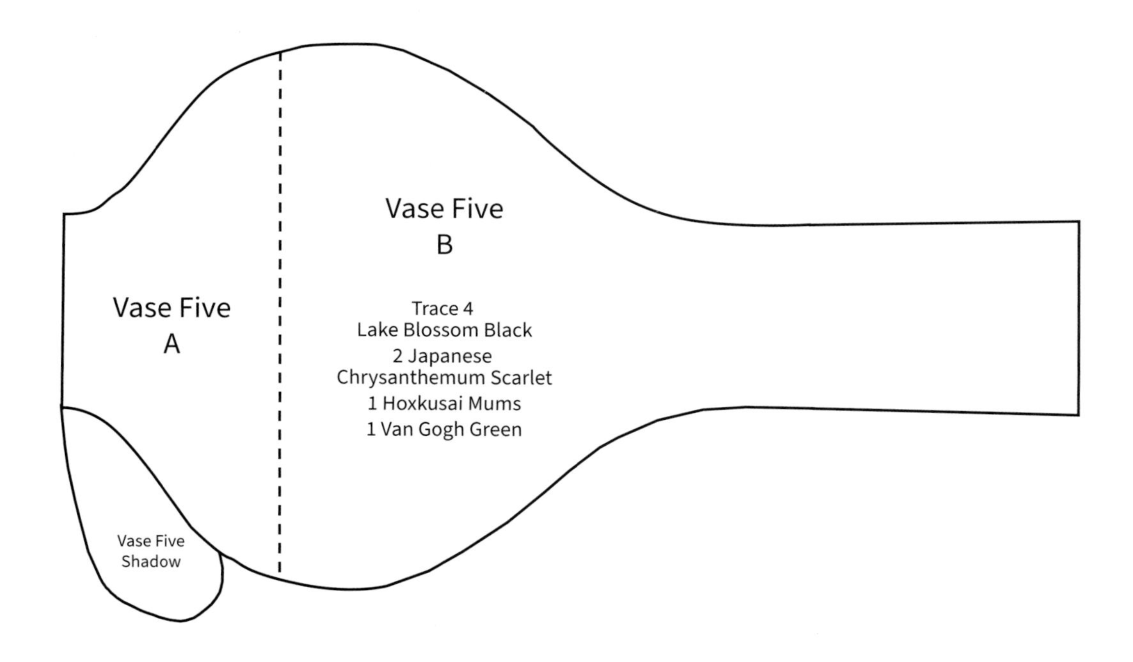

Note there is no seam allowance on the templates! Prepare the templates and fabric according to your preferred method of appliqué.
Pay attention to the direction of the motifs in each fabric. Fussy cut each vase, adding ¼ inch (.6 cm) beyond the template if doing turned edge appliqué.

This quilt was made by cutting out freezer paper templates with no seam allowance and then cutting out the vase fabric with ¼ inch (0.6 cm) seam allowance added. The edges were turned under, using freezer paper to guide, then starched. Then the vases were machine appliquéd using a dark blue thread.
Vase Template 1: Cut 4 Shaggy Black.
Vase Template 2: Cut 2 Van Gogh Green.
Vase Template 3: Cut 4 Cactus Flower Tawny.
Vase Template 4: Cut 4 Cactus Flower Cool, 4 Hokusai's Mums, and 2 Van Gogh Blue.
Vase Template 5: Cut 4 Lake Blossom Black, 2 Japanese Chrysanthemum Scarlet, 1 Hokusai's Mum, and 1 Van Gogh Green

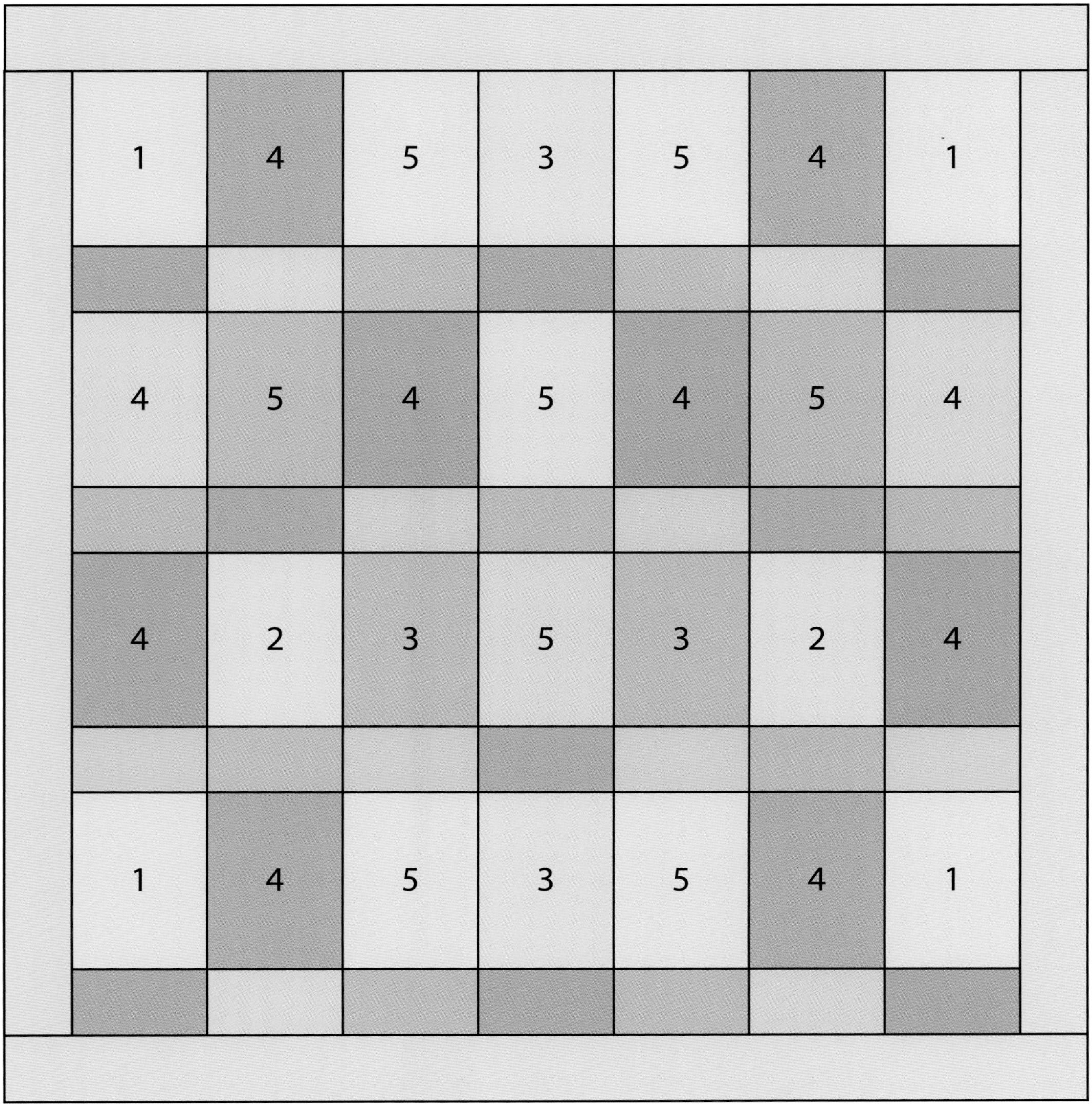

1 4 5 3 5 4 1

4 5 4 5 4 5 4

4 2 3 5 3 2 4

1 4 5 3 5 4 1

Backing:

Cut 3 lengths measuring approximately 40 × 103 inches (102 × 260 cm). Remove selvages. Sew together. Trim backing to approximately 102 × 110 inches (260 × 280 cm)

Binding:

Cut 11 strips measuring 2½ inches (6 cm) wide from selvage to selvage. Remove selvage. Sew end to end.

ASSEMBLING

Use the photo of the quilt as a guide to pair the wall and floor fabrics. Sew the wall to the floor. Make 18 blocks. Press the seam allowance open.

Appliqué a shadow to the base of each vase. Follow the photo to pair up the vases with the backgrounds.

Appliqué a vase to each background. Optional: Cut the backing away from behind each vase.

Arrange the blocks into 4 rows with 7 blocks each. Sew the blocks together in rows. Sew the rows together.

Sew the shorter border lengths to the sides. Sew the longer border lengths to the top and bottom.

FINISHING

Press. Layer top, batting, and back. Baste. Quilt using blue thread, meandering throughout the backgrounds and around flowers in the vases.

Trim. Bind.

AIN'T YOU GOT A VASE?

Any collection of prints in any theme of your choice would work here. Mirror imaging gives a good balance as well as a consistent level of tone. Avoid being too contrasting in your palette and choose a sashing that holds the various elements together. A slightly darker print at the corners helps center the composition as well.

FINISHED SIZE

56 × 56 inches (142 × 142 cm)

FABRIC CHOICES

½ yard (46 cm) for the center square

¼ to ½ yard* (23 to 46 cm) each of 11 prints for the 32 main squares

1⅜ yard (126 cm) for sashing. Paperweight Pastel is used here

⅛ yard* (11.5 cm) for the sashing cornerstones

**If fussy cutting, you may need more yardage.*

Backing:

3¾ yard (3.5 m) of a print in a similar theme

Binding:

½ yard (46 cm)

CUTTING

Center square: Cut a square measuring 16½ × 16½ inches (42 × 42 cm).

Theme blocks: Cut squares measuring 7½ × 7½ inches (19 × 19 cm), for a total of 32 squares. If arranged as in this example, there are 4 identical squares in five of the prints. There are 2 identical squares in six of the prints.

For best visual impact, cut just 2 blocks from each print to begin with. Arrange these on a design wall until figuring out the symmetry you wish to achieve. Then cut the rest as needed.

Fussy cut 12 cornerstone patches measuring 2½ × 2½ inches (6 × 6 cm).

Sashing:

A. Block Sashing: Cut 2 strips measuring 7½ inches (19 cm) wide from selvage to selvage, then crosscut at 2½ inches (6 cm), making 16 sashing rectangles from each strip. 32 sashing rectangles measuring 2½ × 7½ inches (6 × 19 cm) are needed.

B. Center Panel Border Sashing: Cut 2 strips measuring 2½ inches (6 cm) wide from selvage to selvage. Crosscut into 4 rectangles measuring 2½ × 16½ inches (6 × 42 cm) each.

C. Inner Border and Outer Border Sashing: Cut 10 strips measuring 2½ inches (6 cm) wide from selvage to selvage. Remove selvages and sew end to end. Then for the inner borders, cut 4 lengths measuring 34½ inches (87.5 cm). For the outer borders, cut 4 lengths measuring 52½ inches (133 cm).

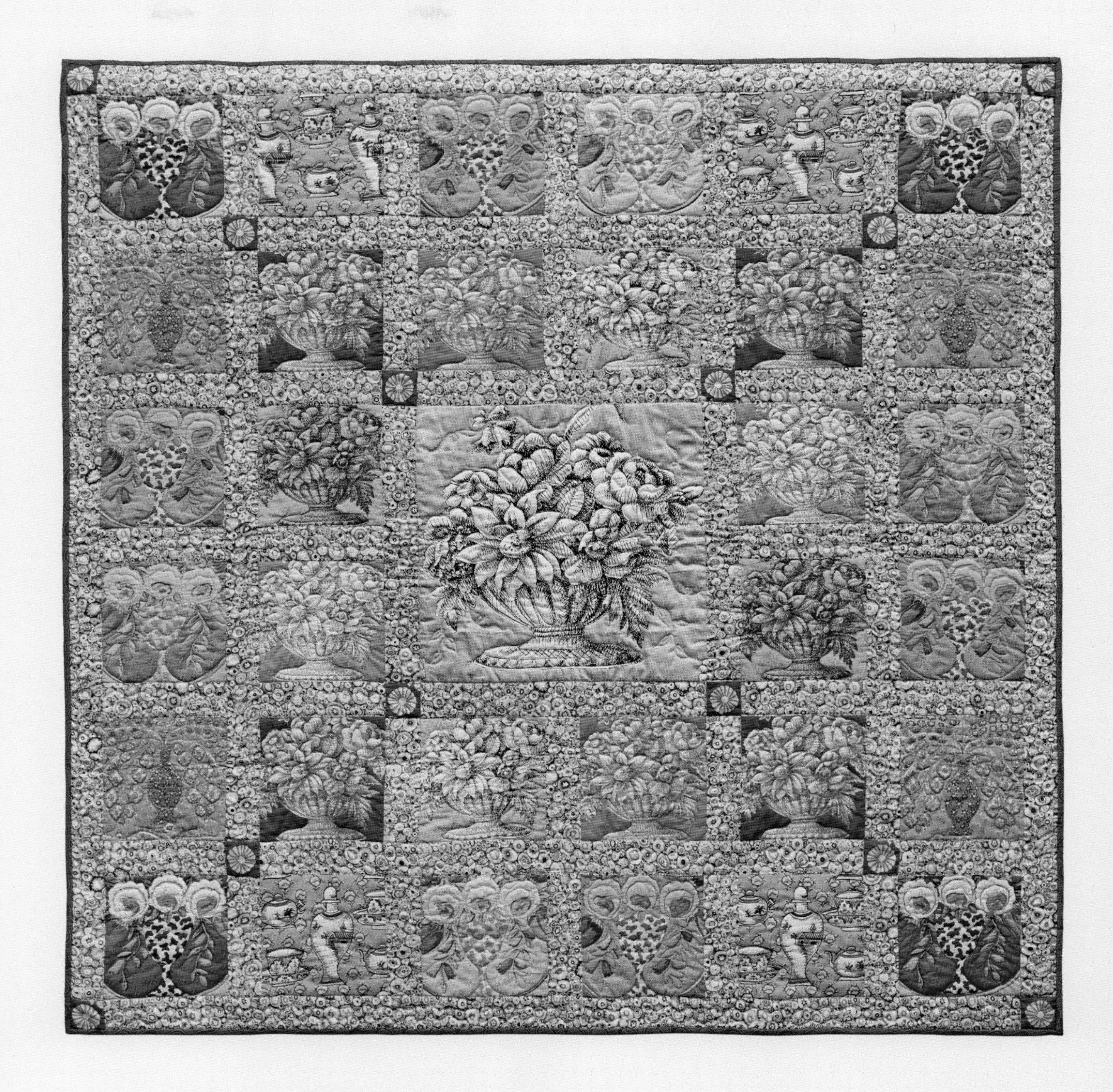

Backing:

Cut 2 lengths measuring approximately 65 inches (165 cm). Remove the selvages and sew together. Trim to approximately 65 × 65 inches (165 × 165 cm).

Binding:

Cut 6 strips measuring 2½ inches (6 cm) wide from selvage to selvage. Remove the selvages. Sew end to end.

ASSEMBLING

Arrange the theme blocks until there is a pleasing symmetrical arrangement. Follow the diagram for the piecing sequence. This pattern is a little tricky because of the borders. If the diagram is followed, there will be no need for partial seams.

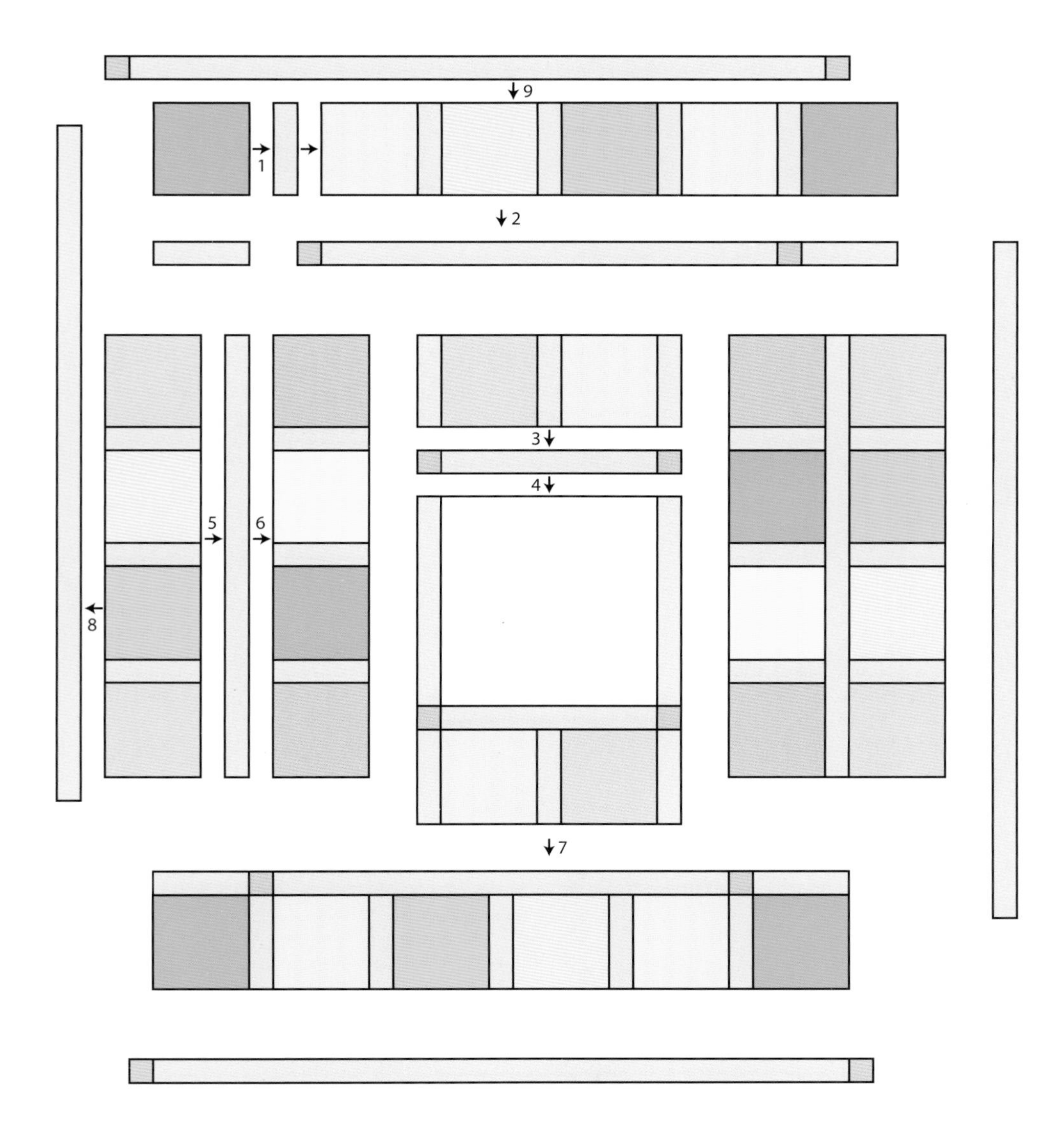

FINISHING

Press. Layer top, batting, and backing. Quilt as desired. Or, using a thread that harmonizes with your colors, meander in the sashings and borders. Quilt around the motifs in your squares.

Trim. Bind.

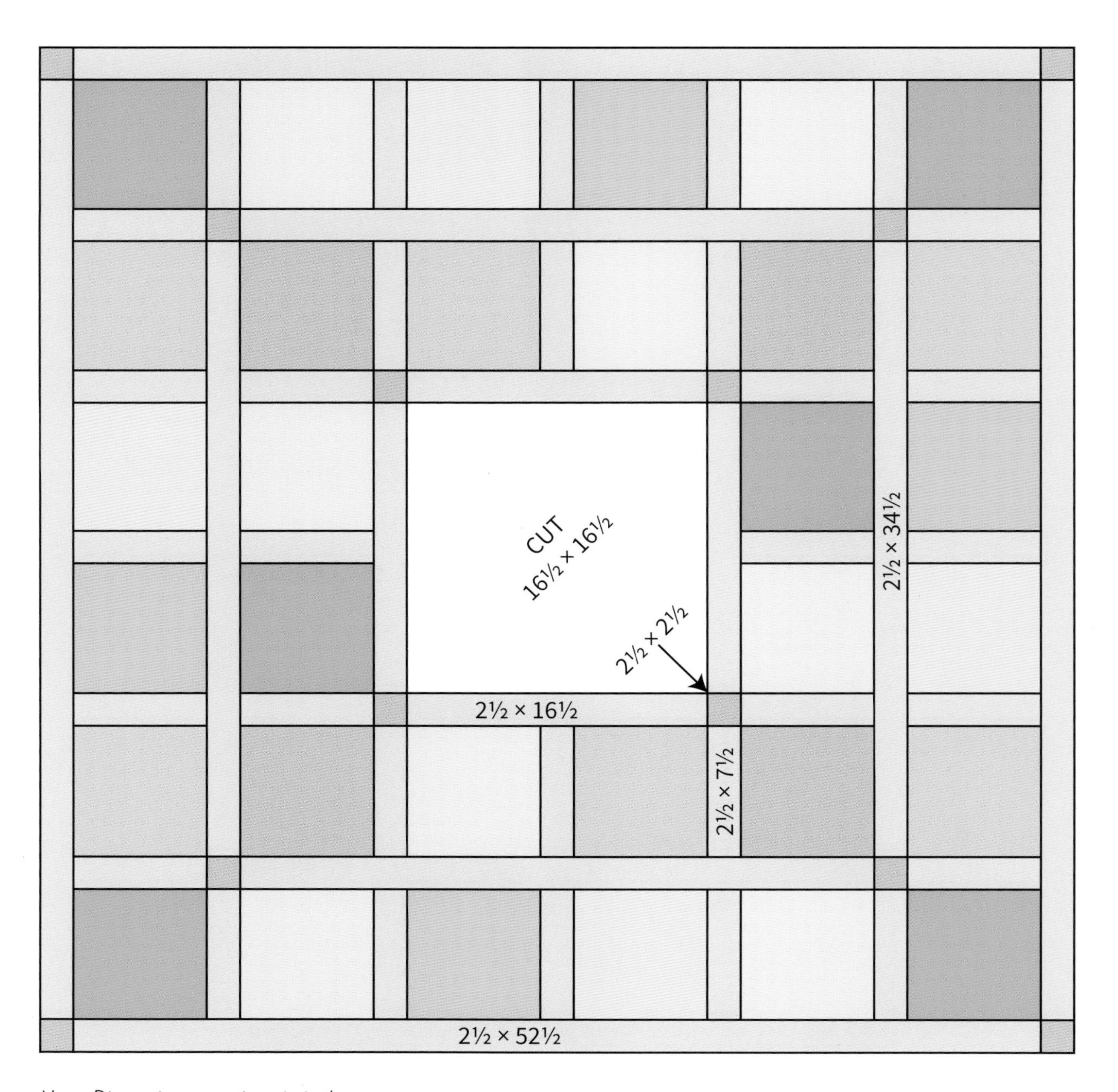

Note: Dimensions are given in inches.

SCRAPPY RICE BOWLS

This version of Rice Bowls is all about circles. Though there is a lot of strong pattern used in this piece, certain elements help it "read." I picked circular flower prints: Spiral Shells, Beach Balls, and my favorite, Oranges. The small prints in the backgrounds and interiors of the bowls are also circular, such as Spots, Paperweight, Buttons, and Onion Rings.

The secret of successful bowls is to have a large-scale exterior that "reads" as a decorated bowl. Bold, larger prints help the active center of the quilt to keep going to its edge. Keeping the backgrounds and bowl interiors small, or often 2-color prints, helps the larger-scale bowls to stand out. The backgrounds are the darkest to help push the bowls forward visually. Keeping all the interiors pale makes for a unity in all the scrappy complexity.

The border really underlines the circular theme with its high-contrast Oranges print. The binding in sharp; black-and-white polka dots are a great finishing detail.

You could of course use many different themes here, perhaps using all Asian-inspired prints. Or using all stripes could be very jazzy. I'd keep large-scale stripes for the bowl exteriors and finer ones for everything else, playing with tonal contrasts in your print selection.

The big, gently curved pieces make this an easy appliqué project. It is your choice on how to do the appliqué. It can be done with raw edge or needle turn, or use any preferred method. This one was done by hand appliqué using the needle turn method.

FINISHED SIZE

67½ × 76 inches
(171.5 × 193 cm)

FABRIC CHOICES

Every fabric in this quilt is from the Kaffe Fassett Collective. All are dotty. The fabrics that are used for the border, sashing, cornerstones, and bowl shadows are currently available. Many of the fabrics used in the bowls and backgrounds are current, but some are older. It isn't necessary to find each fabric and place as in the original. Just collect and use your choice of dotty fabrics.

Outside border:

2 yards (183 cm) Oranges Contrast

Sashing and cornerstones:

1 yard (91 cm) Jumble Black
¼ yard (23 cm) Jumble Bubblegum

There are 20 rice bowls in this pattern.

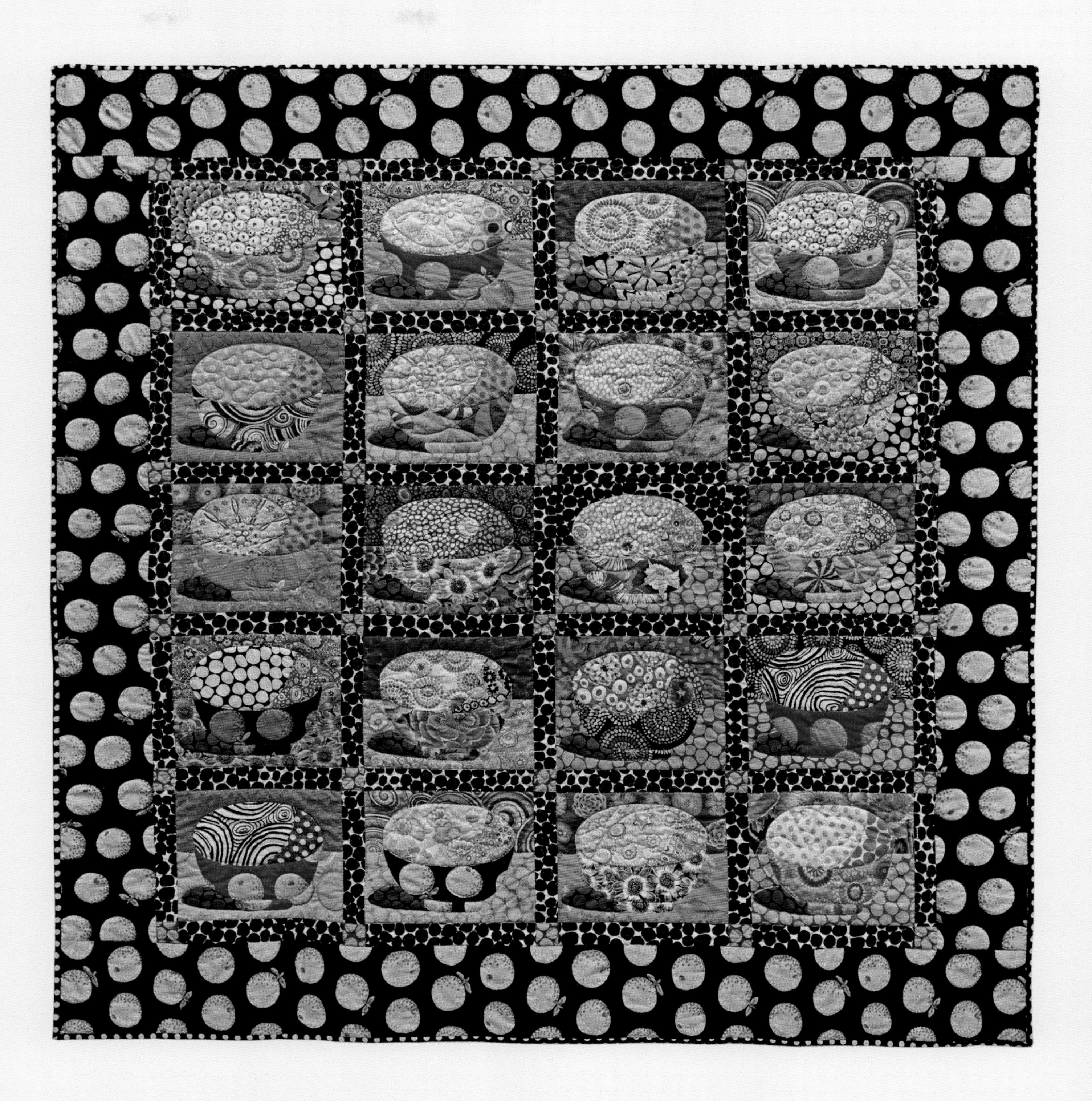

Bowl shadows:
½ yard (46 cm) Jumble Blue

Bowl interiors:
¼ to ½ yard (23 to 46 cm) each white, off-white, and light blue fabrics. Some that were used are Millefiore Pink, Lilac, and Grey; Guinea Flower Mauve and Grey; Roman Glass Pastel; Button Mosaic White; Spot Duck Egg and Sky; Jumble White; Mosaic Circles White; and Onion Rings Black.

Bowl interior shadows:
¼ yard (23 cm) each medium blues, lilacs, and grays. Some that were used are Roman Glass Lavender and Blue, Spot Autumn and Charcoal, Jumble Cobalt, and Guinea Flower Cobalt.

Bowl exterior and foot:
¼ to ½ yard (23 to 46 cm) each medium-toned fabrics with large dots. Some that were used are Oranges Maroon, Purple, Pink, Orange, Lavender, and Lime; Mosaic Circles Black and Pink; and Lucy Grey and Pink.

Background floors:
¼ to ½ yard (23 to 46 cm) each medium-light dotty fabrics. Some that were used are Jumble Duck Egg, Lime, Turquoise, Pink, and Rose; Lucy Magenta; Flower Dot Stone; and Roman Glass Emerald.

Background walls:
¼ to ½ yard (23 to 46 cm) each dark-medium dotty fabrics. Some that were used are Millefiore Aqua, Jumble Purple and Prune, Flower Dot Purple, Roman Glass Purple, and Lucy Lavender.

Backing:
5 yards (4.6 m)

Binding:
¾ yard (68.5 cm) Spot Noir

NOTIONS

Template plastic and/or freezer paper
If doing hand appliqué, we recommend:
Aurifil 80 wt cotton threads
#10 or #11 straw needles
Fine silk pins

Optional:
Fabric glue
Liquid starch

CUTTING

Borders:
From Oranges Contrast, cut 2 lengths measuring 6½ × 68 inches (16.5 × 173 cm) for the top and bottom. Cut 2 lengths measuring 6½ × 64½ inches (16.5 × 164 cm) for the sides.

Floors and rectangles:
Make 20 floor rectangles from an assortment of dotty fabrics. Cut each 6½ × 12½ inches (16.5 × 32 cm).
Make 20 wall rectangles from an assortment of dotty fabrics. Cut each 5½ × 12½ inches (14 × 32 cm).

Sashing:
From Jumble Black, cut 25 rectangles measuring 2 × 11½ inches (5 × 28 cm) for the vertical sashing. Cut 24 rectangles 2 × 12½ inches (5 × 32 cm) for horizontal sashing.

Cornerstones:
From Jumble Bubblegum, cut 30 squares measuring 2 × 2 inch (5 × 5 cm)

Backing:
Cut 2 lengths measuring approximately 84 inches (210 cm). Remove selvages. Sew together making a backing approximately 80 × 84 inches (200 × 210 cm). Trim to approximately 76 × 84 inches (193 × 210 cm).

Binding:
Cut 8 strips 2½ inches (6 cm) wide from selvage to selvage. Remove selvages. Sew end to end.
Prepare templates according to your preferred method of appliqué. Make sure your template remains right side up, because the pieces are not perfectly symmetrical. Note that you can mix up the fabrics, and sometimes bowl fabrics can be backgrounds.
From Jumble Blue, using Template As, cut 20 bowl shadows.
From an assortment of mostly white or pale dotty fabrics, using Template C and adding a seam allowance (unless doing raw edge appliqué), cut 20 bowl interiors.
From an assortment of mostly blue or mauve dotty fabrics, using Template Cs, cut 20 bowl interior shadows.
Cut an assortment of dotty fabrics for the bowl exterior with a matching foot. Make sure not to match up the pattern exactly so that the foot is clearly separate from the bowl. Make 20 of these pairs.
The templates should be enlarged 200%.

ASSEMBLING

Assembling the blocks:

Sew one background wall to one floor wall for each block. Make 20. Press seams open.

Assembling the appliqué:

Do this in any preferred method. Here is how we do it: Prepare each element by turning the edges around freezer paper and, using liquid starch, press firmly to set the edge. Remove the freezer paper. Sew the interior shadow to the interior. Sew the foot to the shadow. Sew the bowl base to the foot and shadow. Sew the bowl base to the bowl interior. Then appliqué the bowl to the background. Cut the backing away from behind the appliqué, leaving approximately a ¼-inch (0.6 cm) seam allowance.

Assembling the top:

Alternate 5 vertical sashing rectangles with 4 blocks. Sew into a row. Make 5 rows.
Alternate 5 cornerstones with 4 longer sashing rectangles to make 6 horizontal sashing strips.
Alternate horizontal sashings with bowl rows. Sew together.

FINISHING

Press. Layer top, batting, and backing. Baste. Quilt around many of the dots in the details and in the backgrounds and border. Trim. Bind.

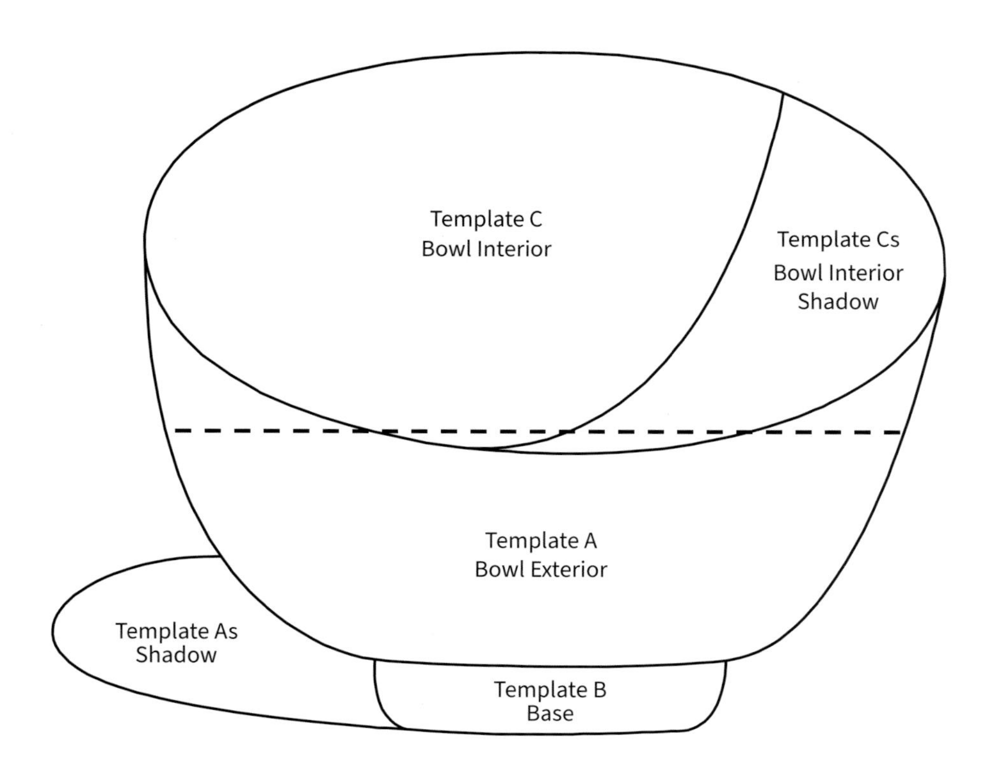

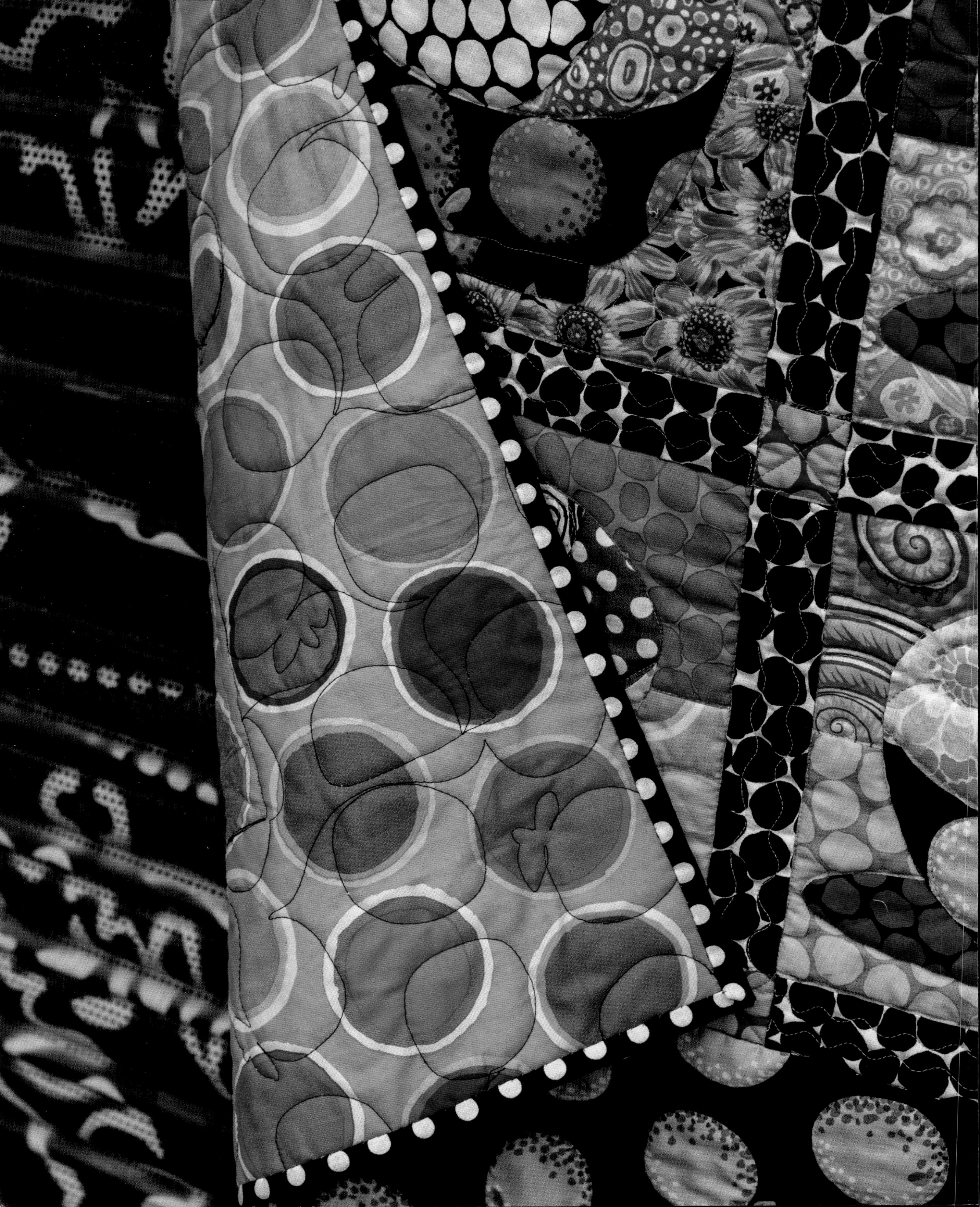

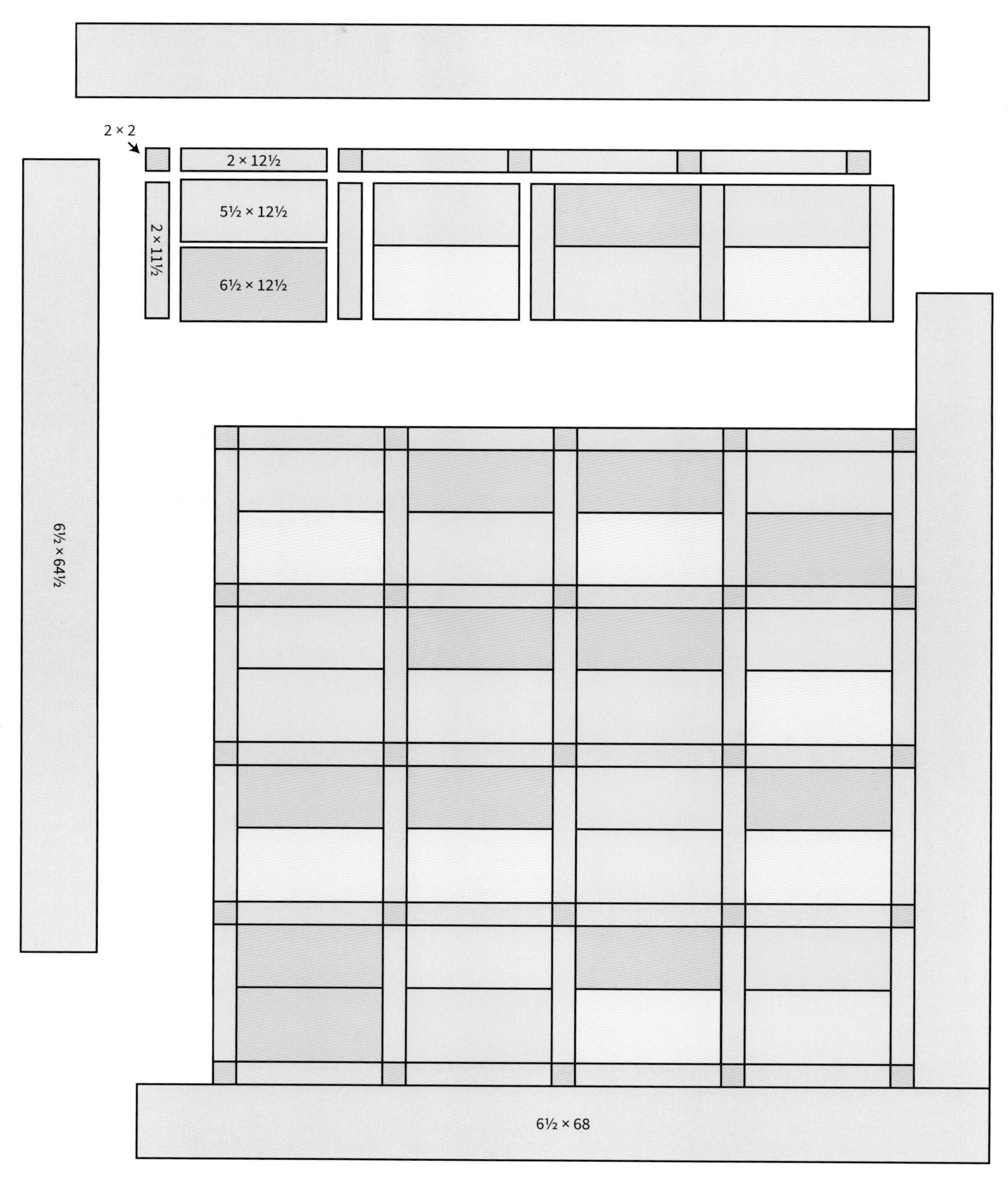

Note: Dimensions are given in inches.

ORGANIC LOG CABIN

Whatever collection of prints you choose, be sure the colors don't vary too much in level—perhaps all darker would be good, or try very faded pastels and soft grays. You could also go wild with jazzy black-and-white large-scale prints with a smattering of high colors.

FINISHED SIZE

52 × 57½ inches
(132 × 146 cm)

FABRIC CHOICES

All of the fabrics used in this quilt came from older Kaffe Fassett Collective stashes. All are medium tones in rust, olive, and gold. Choose scraps or quarter- and half-yard pieces of fabric. "Make do" is how to approach this pattern.

Backing:
3½ yards (3.2 m)

Binding:
½ yard (46 cm)

CUTTING

These are the measurements used to assemble this top. For any length specified, it can be cut from a single fabric or from pieced fabrics.
It may be tempting to just start in the middle, sew a log on, then trim and continue in that manner, but a wonky outcome is likely.

Center:
3½ × 3½ inches (9 × 9 cm)
A: 2 × 3½ inches (5 × 9 cm)
B: 2 × 5 inches (5 × 13 cm)
C: 3 × 5 inches (7.5 × 13 cm)
D: 3 × 7½ inches (7.5 × 19 cm)
E: 3½ × 7½ inches (9 × 19 cm)
F: 3½ × 10½ inches (9 × 26.5 cm)
G: 2 × 10½ inches (5 × 26.5 cm)
H: 2 × 12 inches (5 × 30.5 cm)
I: 2 × 12 inches (5 × 30.5 cm)
J: 6 × 12 inches (15 × 30.5 cm)
K: 6 × 19 inches (15 × 48 cm)
L: 6 × 17½ inches (15 × 44.5 cm)
M: 6 × 24½ inches (15 × 62 cm)
N: 6 × 23 inches (15 × 58.5 cm)
O: 3 × 30 inches (7.5 × 76 cm)
P: 3 × 30 inches (7.5 × 76 cm)
Q: 3 × 28 inches (7.5 × 71 cm)
R: 3 × 28 inches (7.5 × 71 cm)
S: 3 × 35 inches (7.5 × 89 cm)
T: 3 × 30½ inches (7.5 × 77.5 cm)
U: 6 × 37½ inches (15 × 95 cm)
V: 6 × 36 inches (15 × 91.5 cm)
W: 10 × 36 inches (25 × 91.5 cm)
X: 6 × 52½ inches (15 × 133 cm)
Y: 6 × 52½ inches (15 × 133 cm)
Z: 6 × 47 inches (15 × 119 cm)
ZZ: 6 × 58 inches (15 × 147 cm)

Backing:
Cut into 2 lengths measuring approximately 66 × 40 inches (167.5 × 102 cm). Remove selvages and sew together to make a piece that measures approximately 66 × 86 inches (167.5 × 220 cm). Trim to 60 × 65 inches (152 × 165 cm).

Binding:
Cut 6 strips 2½ inches (6 cm) wide from selvage to selvage. Remove selvages. Sew end to end.

ASSEMBLING

Start in the center and follow the diagram. Sew A to the Center, then B, and continue in this manner.

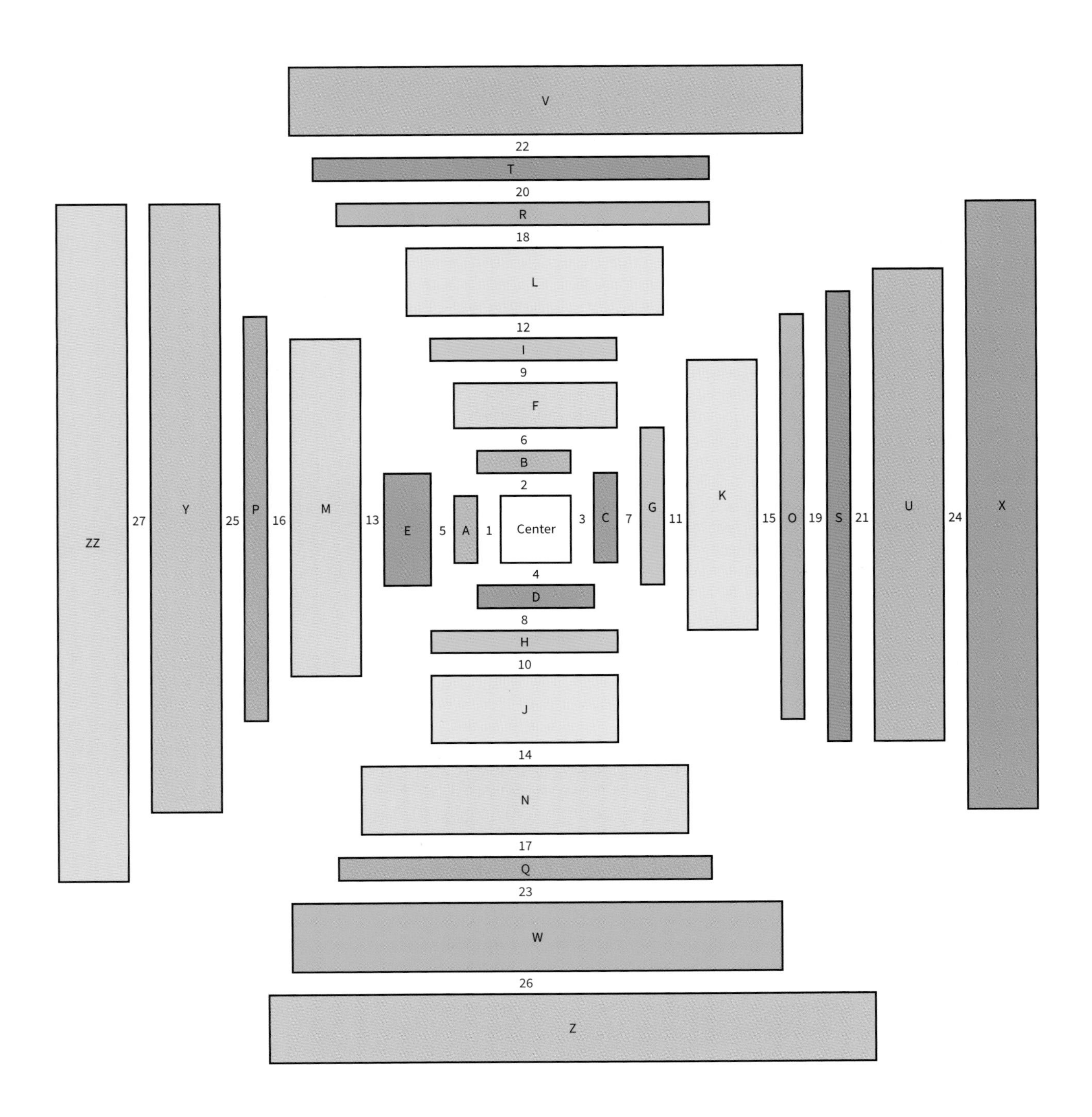

FINISHING

Press. Layer top, batting, and backing. Baste.
Quilt in swirly patterns.
Trim. Bind.

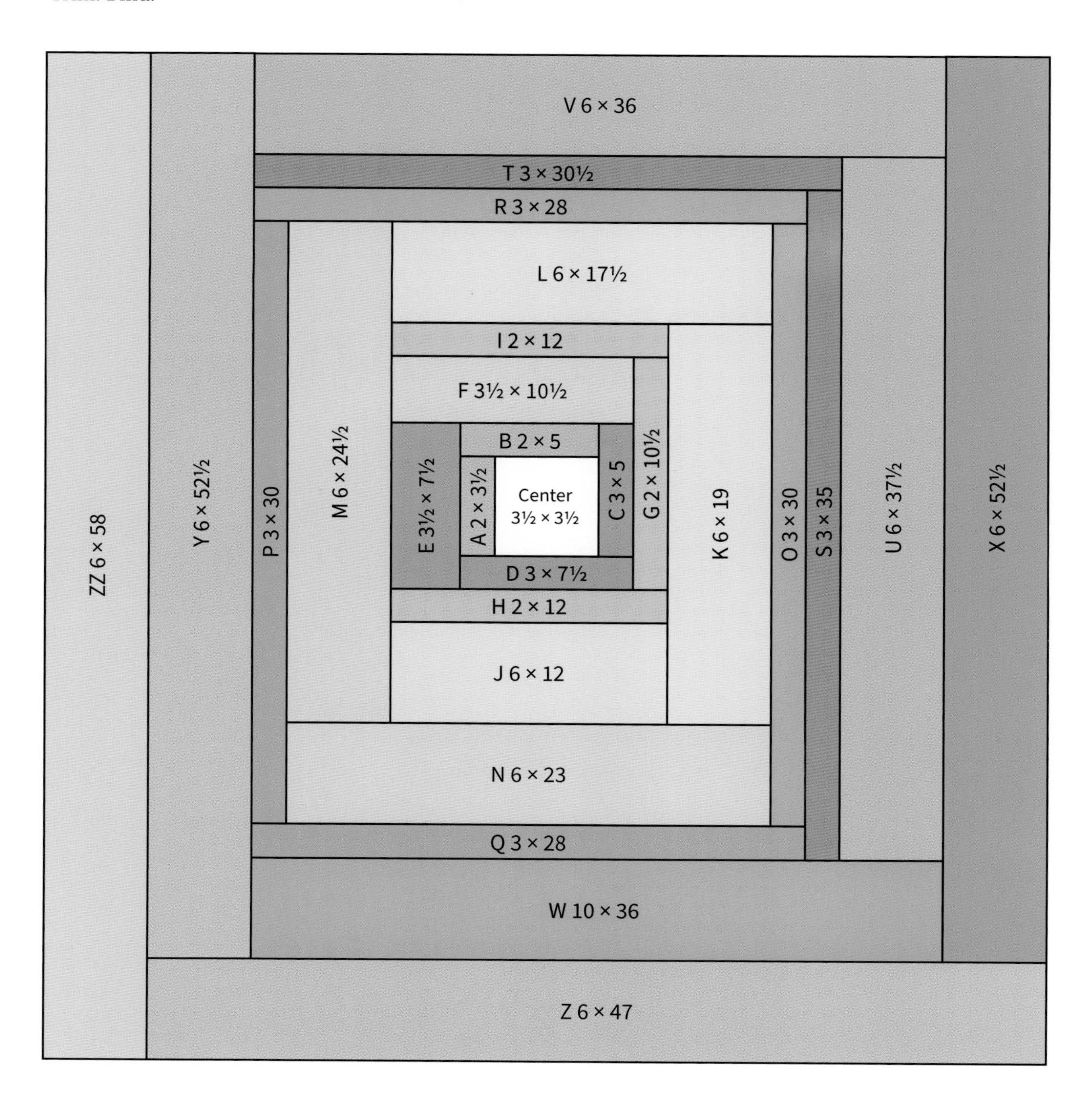

Note: The dimensions represent the cutting measurements, not finished size. Dimensions are given in inches.

ORGANIC SEAHORSES

The repeated shapes on these blocks help you see the rich variety of organic prints. I also limited the palette to these grays, browns, and "greeny"-blues. The base fabrics on each block are more laid back, slightly lighter, and grayed to highlight the brighter, darker "seahorses." The repetition of triangular shapes gives it a formality that I find exciting.

FINISHED SIZE

72 × 84 inches
(183 × 210 cm)
This is a one-patch. All the pieces are half-square triangles.

FABRIC CHOICES

Some of the fabrics we used are Philip Jacobs's Feathers Autumn and Grey, Brassica Grey, Geode Charcoal and Sky, Agate Ochre, and Caladiums Pastel; Kaffe Fassett's Ombre Leaves Gray and Jupiter Purple; and Brandon Mably's Sharks Teeth Carnival and Animal Orange and Sage.

5 dark fabrics—¾ yard (68.5 cm) each
5 light fabrics—¾ yard (68.5 cm) each
2¼ yards (2.1 m) Brassica Grey for border, or another a light fabric

Backing:
5¼ yards (4.8 m)

Binding:
¾ yard (68.5 cm)

CUTTING

Cut border fabric first. Cut 4 lengths of Brassica Grey, measuring 6½ × 72½ inches (16.5 × 184 cm).
From all the other fabrics and the remaining Brassica Grey, cut squares measuring 6⅞ × 6⅞ inches (17.5 × 17.5 cm). Then cut from corner to corner, making 2 triangles from each.

Seahorses:
There are 20 seahorses. Each seahorse has 6 blocks made from half-square triangles.
From the dark fabrics, cut a total of 24 triangles from each.
From the light fabrics, cut between 12–18 triangles from each.

Backing:
Cut 2 lengths measuring approximately 40 × 93 inches (102 × 240 cm). Remove selvages. Sew together to make a backing that measures approximately 80 × 93 inches (200 × 240 cm).

Binding:
Cut 8 strips measuring 2½ inches (6 cm) wide from selvage to selvage. Remove selvages. Sew end to end.

ASSEMBLING

Each seahorse block is made using one dark fabric and one light fabric, 6 triangles of each. Follow the diagram to make a block.

Make 4 blocks from each dark fabric. Choose any light background for each of the dark seahorses. Refer to the diagram to place the dark seahorses so that they are arranged in a very deliberate order.

Sew 5 seahorses in each row. Make 4 rows. Sew rows together.

Sew side borders to the center. Sew the top and bottom borders to the center.

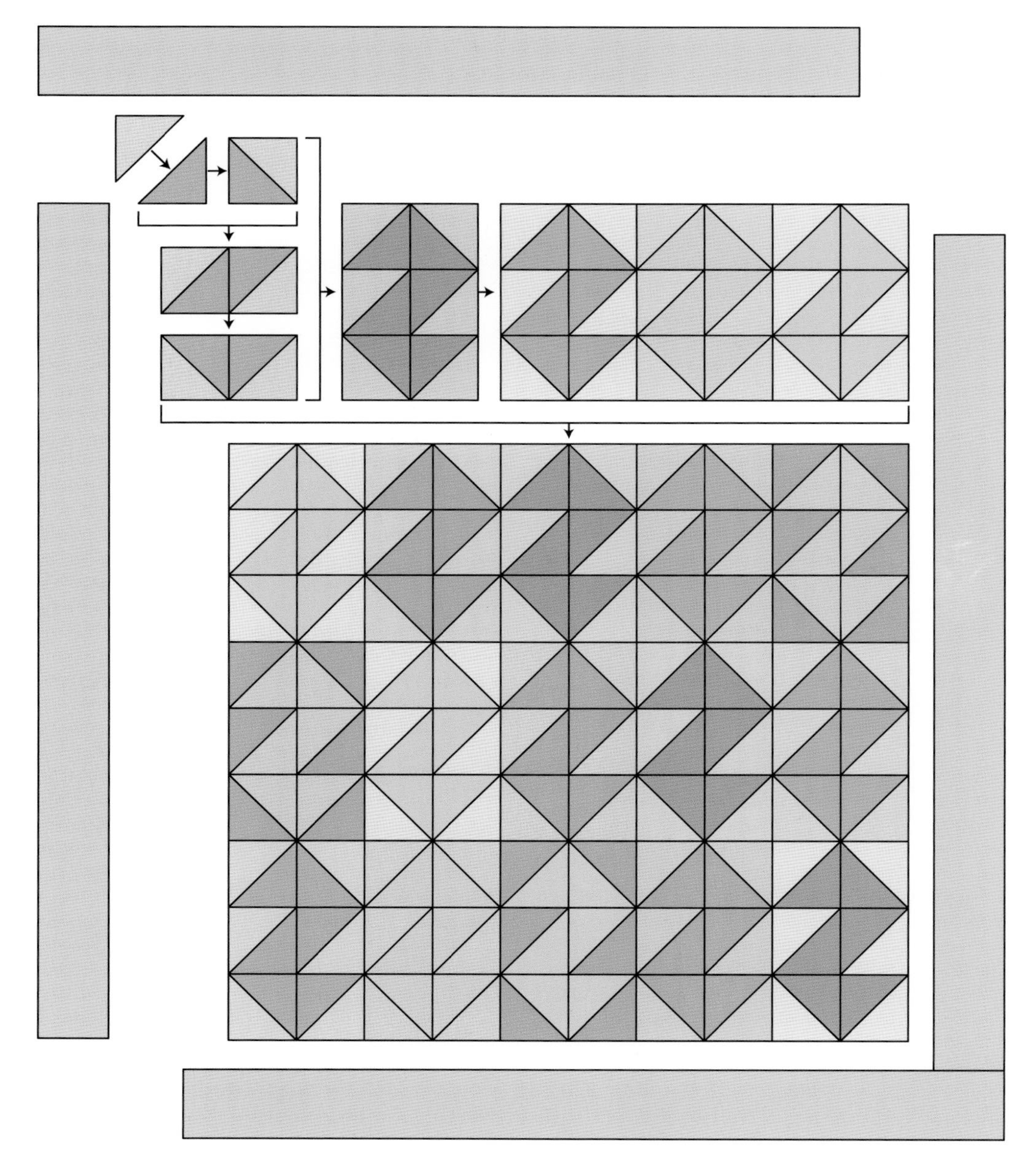

FINISHING

Press. Layer top, batting, and backing. Baste. Using a medium-neutral colored thread, quilt by meandering throughout.

Trim. Bind.

Y OH Y

Choose any prints that have an organic nature in colors that inspire you. Contrast is important here, but colors that enhance each other are what I look for. The scale is bold, which gives the piece its lovely movement.

English Paper Piecing (EPP) is the method used to construct this quilt. Except for the border, the quilt top is constructed by hand. It is a wonderful method to piece odd angles. Enjoy the quiet, slow process of hand-stitching.

FINISHED SIZE

47½ × 62 inches
(120.5 × 157.5 cm)

FABRIC CHOICES

All fabrics are from the Kaffe Fassett Collective.

1 yard (91 cm) Agate Blue
⅝ yard (57 cm) Agate Turquoise
⅝ yard (57 cm) Agate Sky
⅝ yard (57 cm) Agate Pink
⅝ yard (57 cm) Agate Magenta
⅜ yard (34 cm) Agate Ochre
⅜ yard (34 cm) Brassica Magenta
⅜ yard (34 cm) Brassica White
⅜ yard (34 cm) Brassica Grey
1¾ yards (126 cm) Spiral Shells Contrast (includes binding)

Backing:
3½ yards (3.2 m)

EPP SUPPLIES

1 package 3-inch (7.5 cm) half hexagon papers
1 package 3-inch (7.5 cm) half 6-point diamond papers
1 acrylic template for 3-inch (7.5 cm) half hexagons with ⅜-inch (1 cm) seam allowance
1 acrylic template for 3-inch (7.5 cm) half 6-point diamonds with ⅜-inch (1 cm) seam allowance

OTHER NOTIONS

Fabric glue stick
Aurifil 80 wt cotton threads
Size #10 straw needles

CUTTING

Cut the outside borders first. Cut 4 strips 3⅛ inches (8 cm) wide, running the full length of the yardage. Set aside.

For the half hexagons, cut strips 3⅜ inches (8.5 cm) wide from selvage to selvage. Then, using the acrylic half hexagon template, cut the following:

60 Agate Blue
18 Agate Turquoise
18 Agate Sky
18 Agate Pink
18 Agate Magenta
12 Agate Ochre
12 Brassica Magenta
12 Brassica White
12 Brassica Grey
12 Spiral Shells Contrast

Using the 3-inch (7.5 cm) half 6-point diamond template, cut 15 Spiral Shells.

Take one of the half 6-point diamond *papers* and cut in half, making right-side triangle shapes for the quilt corners. Use these papers as templates to cut out the 4 Spiral Shell pieces, with an added ⅜ inch (1 cm) all around for seam allowance. Note that one corner will face one way, and the other will face the opposite direction.

From the remaining Spiral Shells fabric, cut 2½-inch (6 cm) strips and sew end to end to make a binding about 236 inches (6 m) long.

Backing:

Cut 2 lengths measuring approximately 56 inches (142 cm). Remove selvages. Sew together to make a backing that measures approximately 56 × 80 inches (142 × 200 cm). Trim to 56 × 70 inches (142 × 178 cm).

ASSEMBLING

Assembling the Ys:

Although thread basting the papers to the fabrics may be your preferred method, these papers are large, and we found that using a fabric glue stick for basting worked better.

Prepare half hexagon pieces to make each Y shape.

Follow the photo for color choices and the diagram for sewing sequence.

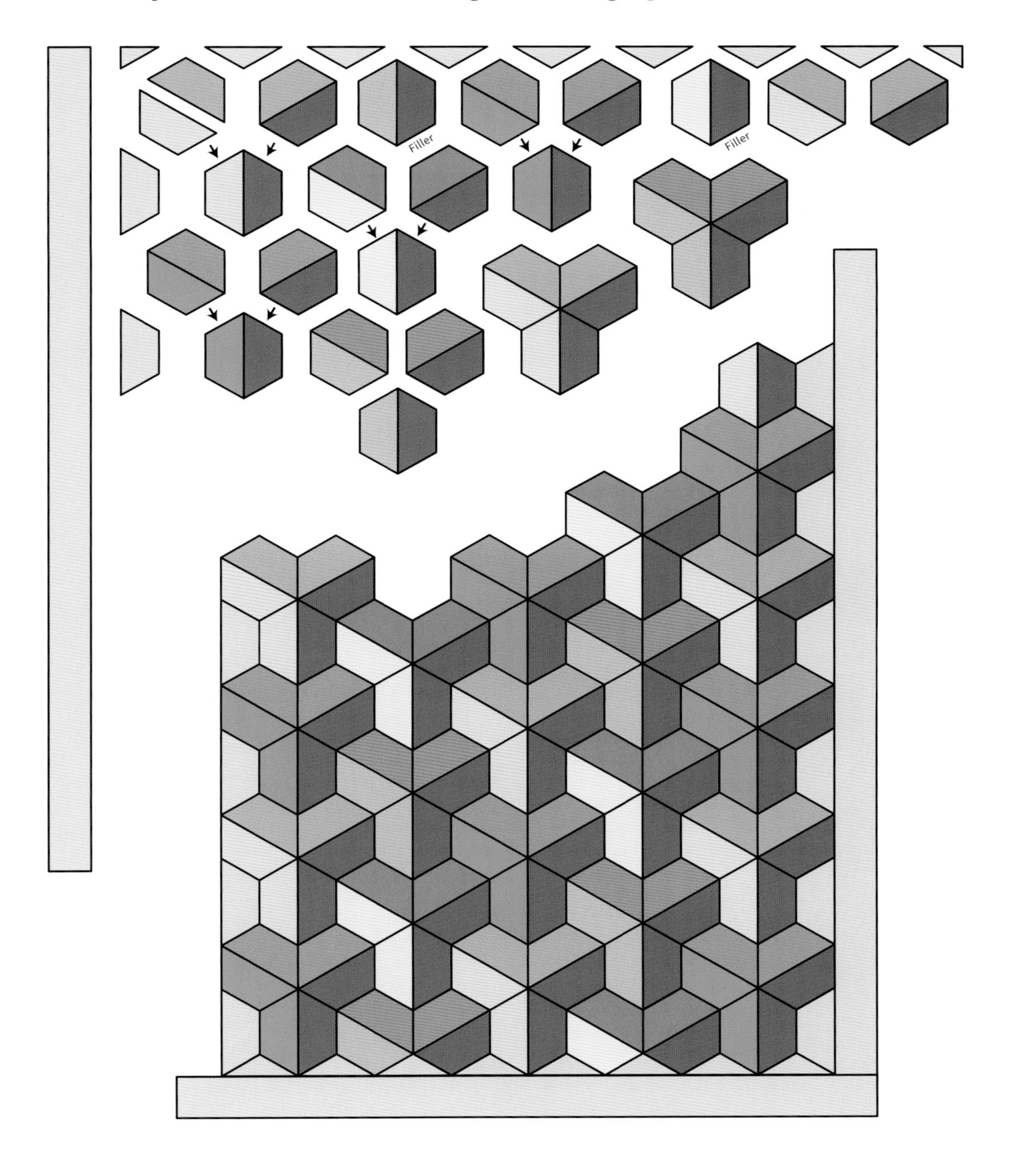

Choose 2 half hexagons for the top of the Y, 2 for the left leg of the Y, and 2 Blue Agate for the right side of the leg. Pair 2 half hexagons to make full hexagons. There will be three pairs that come together to make a Y.
Make 9 Ys with Agate Turquoise, Agate Pink, and Agate Blue.
Make 9 Ys with Agate Sky, Agate Magenta, and Agate Blue.
Make 5 Ys with Agate Ochre, Brassica White, and Agate Blue.
Make 5 Ys with Brassica Magenta, Brassica Grey, and Agate Blue.
There will be 2 partial Ys as fillers at the top and 2 partial Ys at the bottom.
Make 1 top partial with Brassica Grey and Agate Blue.
Make 1 top partial with Brassica White and Agate Blue.
Make 1 bottom partial with Brassica Magenta, Brassica Greg, and Agate Blue.
Make 1 bottom partial with Agate Ochre, Brassica White, and Agate Blue.
Baste 15 Spiral Shells to the 3-inch (7.5 cm) half diamond papers to fill the top and bottom. Baste 2 corner triangles. Baste 12 half hexagons to fill the sides.

Assembling the top:

Sew Ys and fillers together following the diagram.
When each patch is completely sewn to others, remove the paper as you go. This will make it easier to handle as it gets bigger.
When the center is completed, press the edges well, then remove the papers and unfold any tucks along the edges. That creased edge will be the guide for attaching the borders.

Attaching the borders:

The Spiral Shells long strips are to be used for the borders. Sew the side borders on first and then the top and bottom.
Because the exact measurements for your center may differ slightly from ours, measure the length and width of the center to find the measurements for the borders. *Remember the seam allowance is not ¼ inch (.6 cm) but ⅜ inch (1 cm)!*

Our measurements are:

Cut 2 lengths of 3⅛ × 57 inches (8 × 145 cm) for the sides.
Cut 2 lengths 3⅛ × 47½ inches (8 × 120.5 cm) for the top and bottom.

FINISHING

Press. Layer top, batting, and backing. Baste. Quilt either in the ditch or next to seams to enhance the Y shapes.
Trim. Bind.

TUMBLING LEAVES

I've chosen an assortment of medium-pastel prints that gently merge. You could choose any level of color that suits you, perhaps lighter for a delicate look, very dark for drama, or high contrast for a more black-and-white look. Consistent levels in all prints is the key.

FINISHED SIZE

63 × 84 inches
(160 × 210 cm)

FABRIC CHOICES

All these leafy fabrics are from the Kaffe Fassett Collective, so the materials list is very specific. Of course, it would be great for you to do your own original version. Just choose leafy fabrics and one good, strong dark print.

Tops:

⅜ yard (34 cm) Caladiums Dark
¼ yard (23 cm) Coleus Blue
¼ yard (23 cm) Lake Blossoms Black
¼ yard (23 cm) Begonia Leaves Cobalt
⅜ yard (34 cm) Caladiums Red
⅜ yard (34 cm) Brassica Purple
⅜ yard (34 cm) Lotus Leaf Dark
¼ yard (23 cm) Coleus Moss

Left sides:

⅜ yard (34 cm) Brassica Magenta
¼ yard (23 cm) Coleus Teal
⅜ yard (34 cm) Caladiums Bright
¼ yard (23 cm) Caladiums Blue
⅜ yard (34 cm) Brassica Rust
⅜ yard (34 cm) Brassica Orange
⅜ yard (34 cm) Caladiums Gold

Right sides:

1½ yards (137 cm) Spot Black

Border:

2¼ yards (2.1 m) Lotus Leaf Vintage

Backing:

5¼ yards (4.8 m)

Binding:

¾ yard (68.5 cm) Spot Indigo

NOTIONS

Template plastic or a rotary ruler with 60-degree angle lines
Aurifil 12 wt thread in bright colors

CUTTING

Note that the same fabric for the top and for the left side are used in each column of tumbling blocks.

For the full-size diamonds, cut strips measuring 5 inches (13 cm) wide from selvage to selvage. Then, using Template A, cut the following number of parallelograms:
Cut 54 Spot Black
Cut 10 Brassica Magenta
Cut 5 Coleus Teal
Cut 10 Caladiums Bright
Cut 5 Caladiums Blue
Cut 8 Brassica Rust
Cut 8 Brassica Orange
Cut 8 Caladiums Gold.
For the half-diamonds (triangles), cut strips measuring 5¼ inches (13 cm) wide from selvage to selvage. Then, using Template B, cut the following number of triangles:
Cut 20 Caladiums Dark
Cut 10 Coleus Blue
Cut 10 Lake Blossoms Black
Cut 10 Begonia Leaves Cobalt
Cut 18 Caladiums Red
Cut 16 Brassica Purple
Cut 16 Lotus Leaf Dark
Cut 8 Coleus Moss.
From template C, cut the following:
Cut 6 Spot Black
Cut 2 Brassica Purple
Cut 1 Caladiums Red
Cut 2 Lotus Leaf Dark
Cut 1 Coleus Moss.

From Template C reverse, cut the following:
Cut 2 Brassica Purple
Cut 1 Caladiums Red
Cut 2 Lotus Leaf Dark
Cut 1 Coleus Moss
Cut 2 Brassica Rust
Cut 2 Brassica Orange
Cut 2 Caladiums Gold.

Borders:

From Lotus Leaf Vintage, cut 2 lengths measuring 5½ × 74 inches (14 × 188 cm) for the sides.
Cut 2 lengths measuring 5½ × 63 inches (14 × 160 cm) for the top and bottom.

Backing:

Cut 2 lengths measuring approximately 92 inches (230 cm) long.
Remove selvages.
Sew together making a backing that measures approximately 80 × 92 inches (200 × 230 cm). Trim to approximately 72 × 92 inches (183 × 230 cm).

Binding:

Cut 8 strips measuring 2½ inches (6 cm) wide from selvage to selvage.
Remove selvages.
Sew end to end.

ASSEMBLING

It is best to arrange the pieces on a design wall to keep track of the sewing sequence. Because the top of each tumbling block is split into two triangles, there are no set-in seams. The pieces are sewn together in columns. Use the photo and diagram to see the sewing sequence. Sew 12 columns. Sew the columns together. Sew the longer border lengths to the sides. Sew the shorter border lengths to the top and bottom.

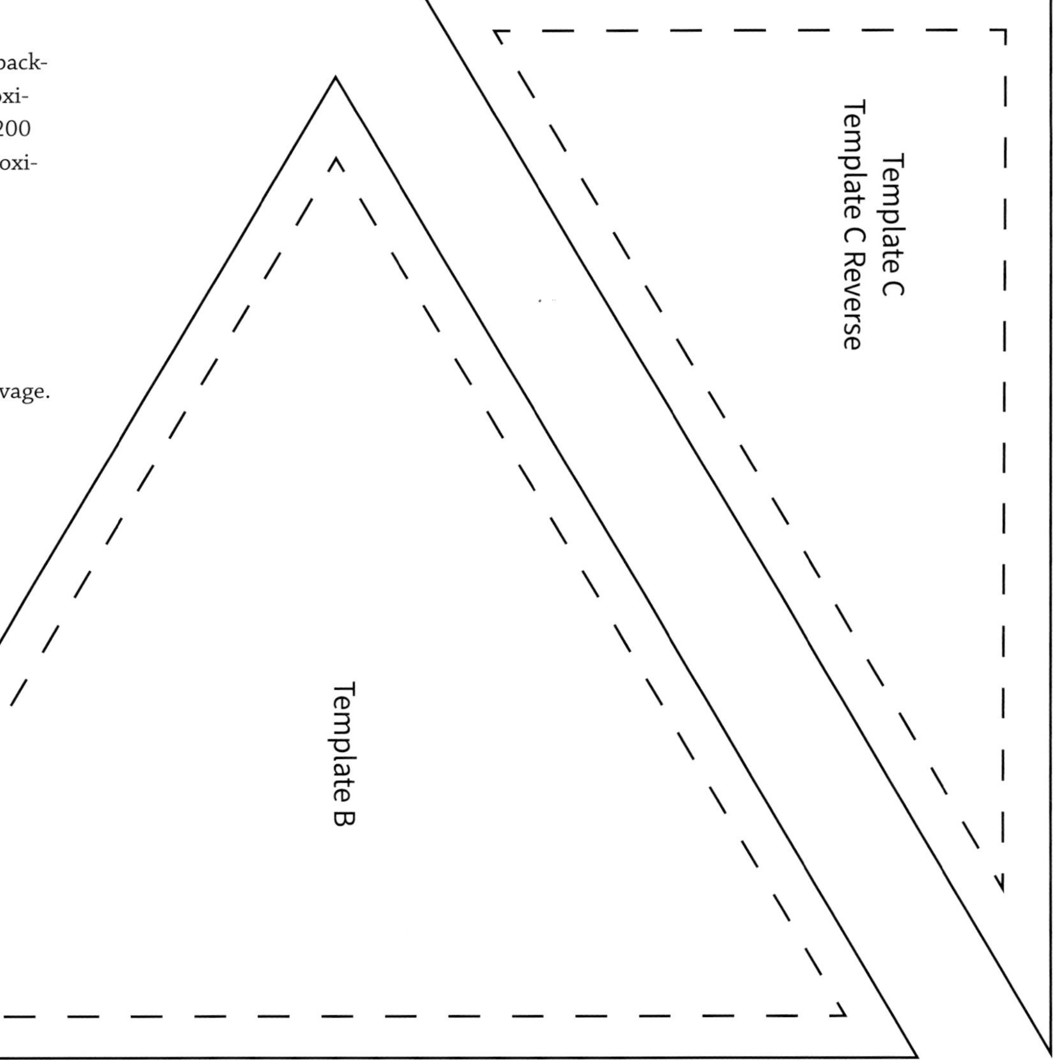

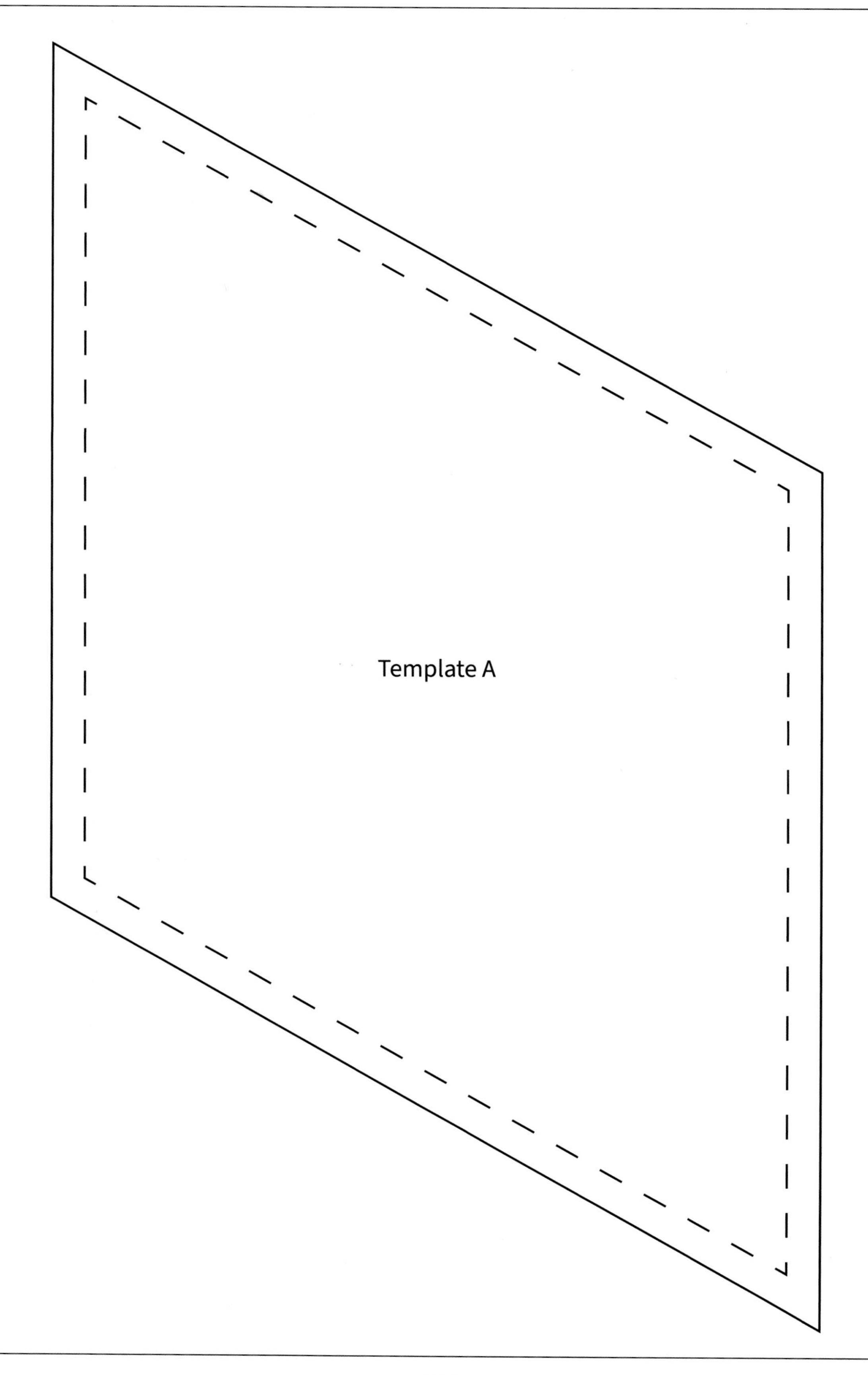
Template A

FINISHING

Press. Layer top, batting, and backing. Baste. Hand-quilt using big stitches about ½ inch (1.3 cm) from the edge of each tumbling block, and another row of stitching about 1 inch (2.5 cm) from the first line of stitching. This will make 2 hexagon shapes. Hand-quilt lines in the border.

Trim. Bind.

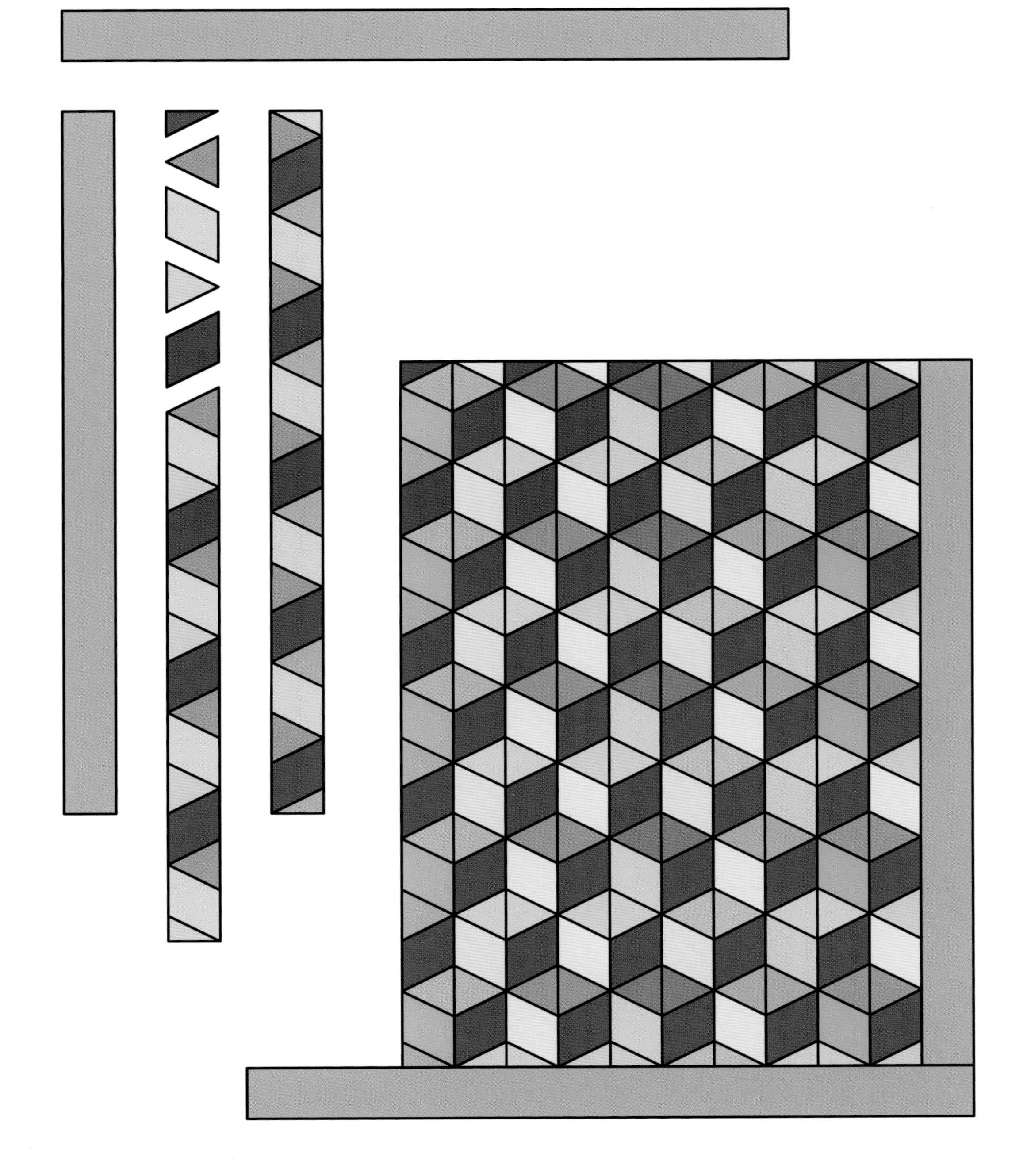

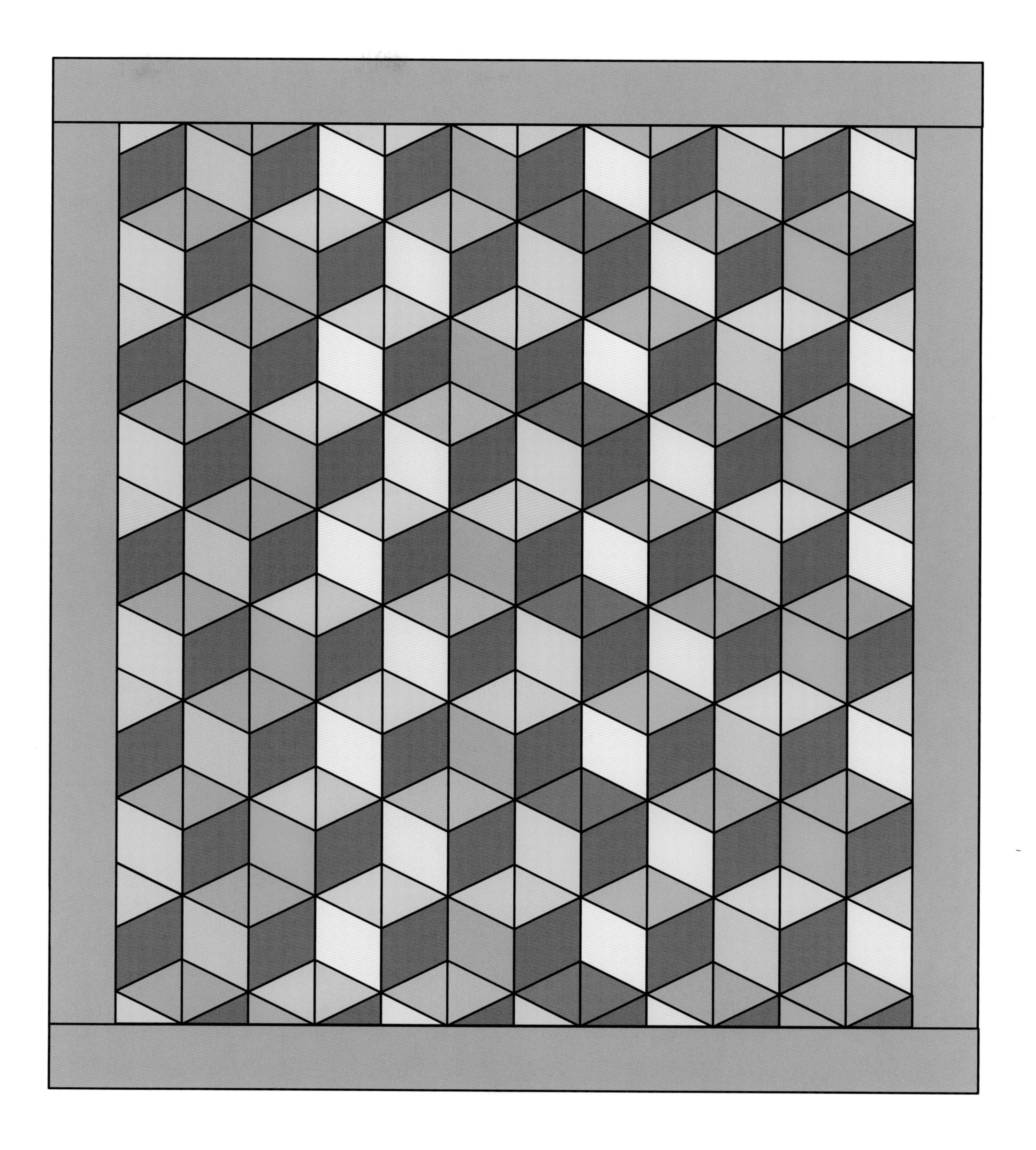

SALAD DAYS

Choose your color level and have as many leafy prints as you can. Large-scale is important, especially with your center, so the whole quilt has a lively open movement. The mirroring of blocks really does the work of holding it all together.

FINISHED SIZE

67½ × 75 inches
(171.5 × 190.5 cm)

FABRIC CHOICES

Some of the Kaffe Fassett Collective fabrics used in this quilt are Banana Tree, Animal, Lake Blossoms, Coleus, Brassica, Lotus Leaf, and Climbing Geraniums. All of the fabrics making up this summery Salad Days pattern are bright pastels.

¼ to ½ yard (23 to 46 cm) of at least fifteen different flower- or leaf-designed fabrics in bright pastels

One piece measuring at least 18 × 26 inches (46 × 66 cm), for the featured center panel

⅜ yard (34 cm) of a leafy, aqua, small-scale print for the center inner border

¼ yard (23 cm) of a green, medium-scale print for the center outer border

2 yards (183 cm) Spot Periwinkle for the Snowball corners

Backing:

4¾ yards (4.3 m)

Binding:

¾ yard (68.5 cm) same fabric as center outer border

CUTTING

Center:

Cut the center panel 17 inches wide × 24½ inches (43 × 62 cm) long.

Inner-center border:

Cut 4 strips measuring 2½ inches (6.5 cm) wide from selvage to selvage. Trim 2 lengths measuring 24½ inches (62 cm) for the sides. Trim 2 lengths measuring 21 inches (53 cm) for the top and bottom.

Outer-center border:

Cut 4 strips measuring 1½ inches (3.8 cm) wide from selvage to selvage. Trim 2 lengths measuring 28½ inches (72 cm) for the sides. Trim 2 lengths measuring 23 inches (58 cm) for the top and bottom.

Snowballs:

Note that the arrangement of the Snowballs is symmetrical. So, for example, if you choose a fabric to be used in one corner, it will be the same fabric for the other three corners.

Cut each Snowball square 8 × 8 inches (20 × 20 cm). Cut a total of 78 squares.
For the Snowball corners, cut 23 strips measuring 2¾ inches (7 cm) wide from selvage to selvage. Crosscut at 2¾ inches (7 cm), making 14 squares from each strip. A total of 312 squares is needed.

Backing:

Cut 2 lengths measuring approximately 83 inches (211 cm) long. Remove selvages. Sew together, making a backing that measures approximately 80 × 83 inches (200 × 210 cm). Trim to approximately 76 × 83 inches (193 × 210 cm).

Binding:

Cut 8 strips measuring 2½ inches (6.5 cm) wide from selvage to selvage. Remove selvages. Sew end to end.

ASSEMBLING

Assembling the center:

Sew the longer center inner border strips to the sides of the center. Sew the shorter strips to the top and bottom. Repeat with the center outer border strips.

Assembling the top:

Make Snowballs. Every Snowball has one 8-inch (20 cm) square and four 2¾-inch (7 cm) Spot Periwinkle squares. Follow diagram and make 78 Snowball blocks.

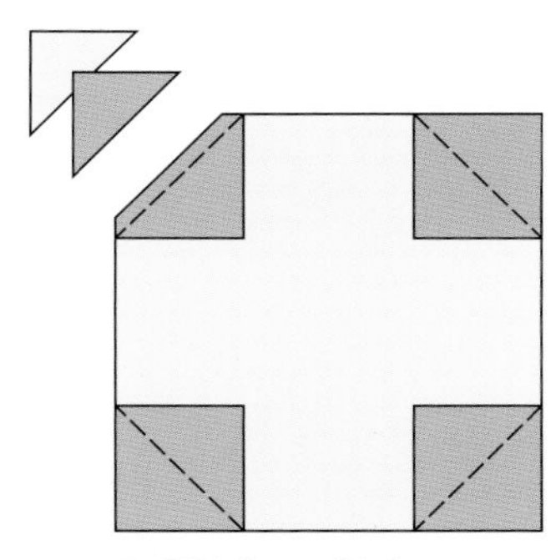

1. Stitch and trim

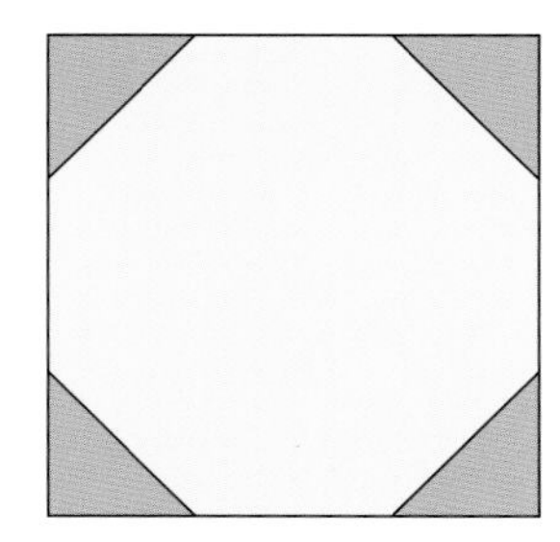

2. Press open

On either side of the center panel, make 4 rows of 3 Snowballs each for each side.
Sew together making the units 3 Snowballs across, 4 rows down.
Sew the side Snowball units to the center panel. Sew the top units to the center.
Sew the bottom units to the center.

FINISHING

Press. Layer top, bottom, and backing. Baste. Quilt around the details in the blossoms. Trim. Bind.

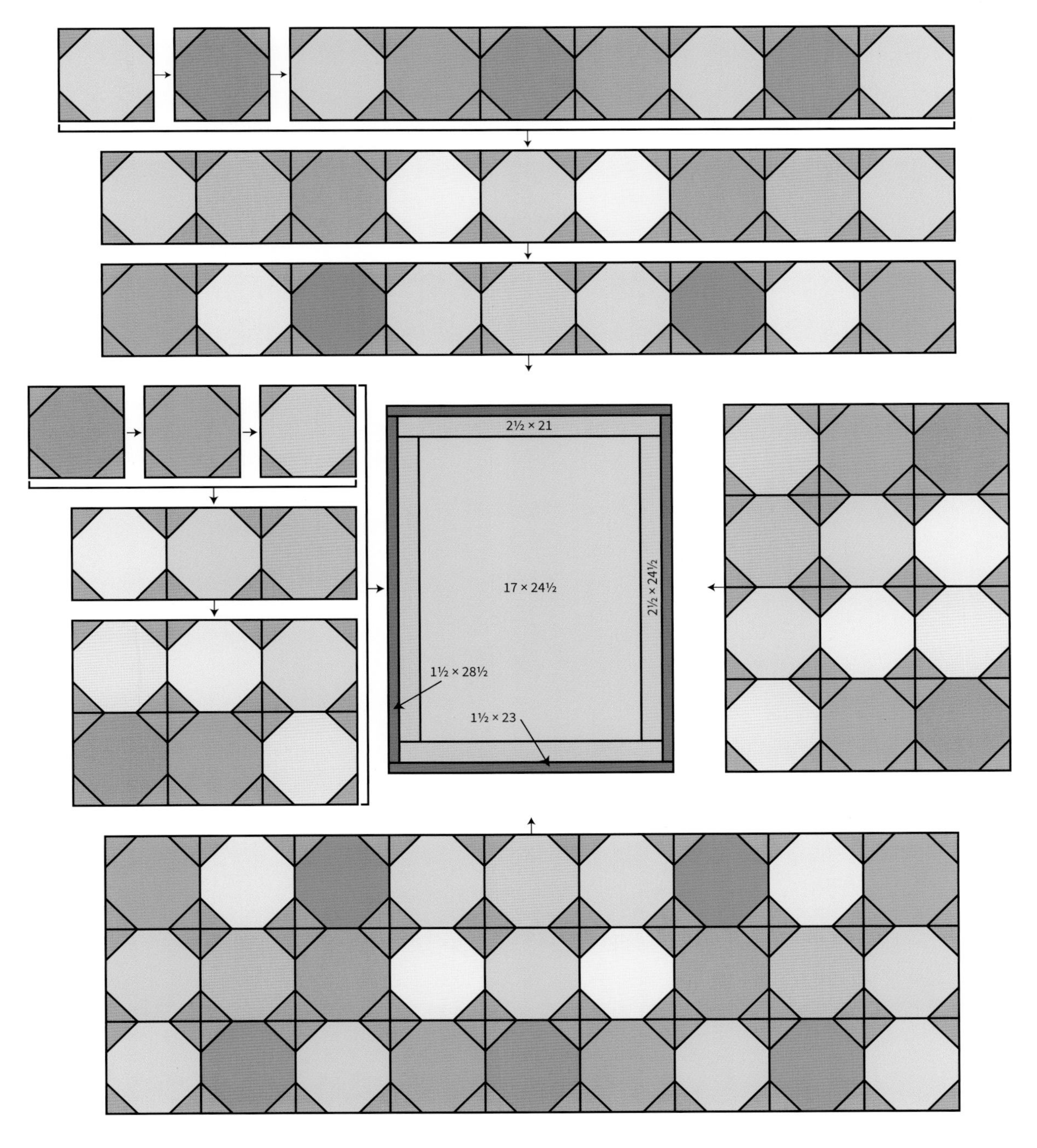

Note: Dimensions are given in inches.

MONKEY WRENCH

This quilt is made entirely in prints from the Kaffe Fassett Collective that are readily available, but if you want a different look, you could use closer, similarly colored prints that make your overall effect a little less defined. The layout almost disappears in a softer coloring, which could be quite mysterious.

FINISHED SIZE

65 × 75 inches
(165 × 190.5 cm)

FABRIC CHOICES

Darks:

- ½ yard (46 cm) Millefiore Dark
- ½ yard (46 cm) Jumble Lapis
- ½ yard (46 cm) Jumble Salmon
- ⅜ yard (34 cm) Roman Glass Purple
- ⅜ yard (34 cm) Guinea Flower Purple
- 2 yards (183 cm) (includes border) Guinea Flower Black

Lights:

- ½ yard (46 cm) Jumble Duck Egg
- ⅜ yard (34 cm) Flower Dot Blue
- ⅜ yard (34 cm) Paperweight Blue
- ¼ yard (23 cm) Guinea Flower Cobalt
- ⅜ yard (34 cm) Guinea Flower Pink
- ⅜ yard (34 cm) Spot Sapphire
- ¼ yard (23 cm) Millefiore Dusty
- ⅜ yard (34 cm) Moss Flower Blue

Background:

¾ yard (68.5 cm) Jumble Blue

Backing:

4¾ yards (4.3 m)

Binding:

¾ yard (68.5 cm) Spot Sapphire

CUTTING

Cut the borders first.

From Guinea Flower Black, cut 4 lengths measuring 5½ × 65½ inches (14 × 166 cm).

There are 25 monkey wrench blocks.

For each "wrench," cut 4 squares measuring 3 × 3 inches (7.5 × 7.5 cm). Cut 2 squares measuring 5⅞ × 5⅞ inches (15 × 15 cm), then cut each from corner to corner, making 2 triangles from each square. Cut 1 square measuring 5½ × 5½ inches (14 × 14 cm).

Cut 3 "wrenches" each from:

Millefiore Dark, Jumble Lapis, Jumble Salmon, and Jumble Duck Egg.

Cut 2 "wrenches" each from:

Roman Glass Purple, Guinea Flower Purple, Guinea Flower Black, Flower Dot Blue, Paperweight Blue, Guinea Flower Pink, Spot Sapphire, Moss Flower Blue.

Cut 1 "wrench" each from:

Guinea Flower Cobalt and Millefiore Dusty.

Background:

From Jumble Blue, cut 11 squares measuring 5⅞ × 5⅞ inches (15 × 15 cm), then cut each from corner to corner, making 2 triangles from each square. Cut 22 rectangles measuring 3 × 5½ inches (7.5 × 19 cm). Cut 4 squares measuring 3 × 3 inches (7.5 × 7.5 cm).

Backing:

Cut 2 lengths measuring approximately 83 inches (211 cm) long. Remove selvages. Sew together making a backing that measures approximately 80 × 83 inches (200 × 210 cm). Trim to approximately 73 × 83 inches (185.5 × 211 cm).

Binding:

Cut 8 strips measuring 2½ inches (6.5 cm) wide from selvage to selvage. Remove selvages. Sew end to end.

ASSEMBLING

All of the "wrenches" are interconnected, so following the diagram exactly is necessary.

Using the diagram, piece into squares and then sew the pieced squares together making rows of 11 pieced squares. There will be 13 rows. Sew the rows together.

Sew 2 borders to the sides, then sew the top and bottom borders to the center.

FINISHING

Press. Layer top, batting, and backing. Baste. Quilt using blue thread and meander throughout. Trim. Bind.

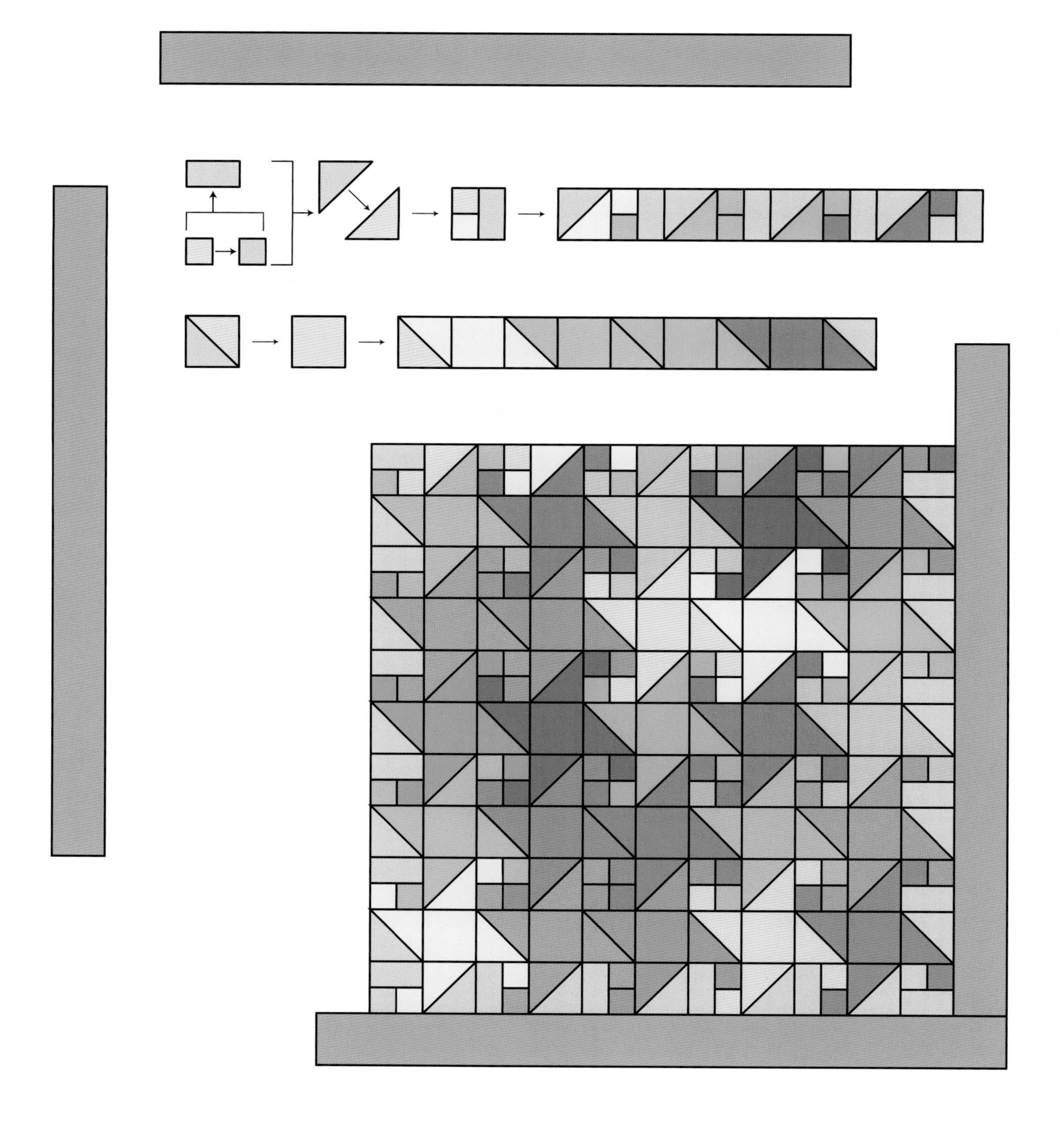

SUGAR CUBES

I feel clearly defined prints of medium-to-small scale are needed to give each part movement. Of course, if you like a flatter look, solids or close tonal prints would give you a sharper, boxy structure.

FINISHED SIZE

78 × 78 inches (198 × 198 cm)

FABRIC CHOICES

All the fabrics are from the Kaffe Fassett Collective. Many are classics and easily sourced. It is not necessary to make this quilt with these exact fabrics. Rather, you can choose dotty-themed fabrics in sweet pastels and a bit of black and white.

Scraps to ½ yard (46 cm)

- Jumble Scarlet, Moss, Tangerine, Turquoise, Cobalt, Rose, Duck Egg, and Bubblegum
- Spot White, Merlot, Mauve, Sky, and China Blue
- Paperweight Pastel
- Roman Glass Emerald and Lavender
- Chips Fog
- Sharks Teeth Pine and Carnival
- Garlands Blue
- Hydrangea Grey
- Button Mosaic White
- Guinea Flower Grey

1½ yards (137 cm) Moss Flower White

Backing:
6¼ yards (5.7 m)

Binding:
¾ yard (68.5 cm) Jumble Cobalt

CUTTING

Cut the borders first.

From Moss Flower, cut 8 strips measuring 4½ inches (11.5 cm) wide from selvage to selvage. Remove selvages and sew end to end. Cut 2 lengths measuring 78½ inches (199 cm) for the top and bottom borders. Cut 2 lengths measuring 70½ inches (179 cm) for the side borders. Use the remaining Moss Flower for the log cabins.

Made from an assortment of fabrics, this is a scrappy quilt. There is no need to put fabrics in the same place as the original. Cut 49 squares measuring 2½ × 2½ inches (6.5 × 6.5 cm) for the block centers.

Cut all remaining fabrics into strips measuring 1½ inches (4 cm) wide. For each block, cut sets of 4 strips in the same fabric following these rounds:

Round 1—cut 2 measuring 2½ inches (6.5 cm); cut 2 measuring 4½ inches (11.5 cm).

Round 2—cut 2 measuring 4½ inches (11.5 cm); cut 2 measuring 6½ inches (16.5 cm).

Round 3—cut 2 measuring 6½ inches (16.5 cm); cut 2 measuring 8½ inches (21.5 cm).

Round 4—cut 2 measuring 8½ inches (21.5 cm); cut 2 measuring 10½ inches (26.5 cm).

Backing:

Cut 2 lengths measuring approximately 86 inches (220 cm) long. Cut 1 length approximately 44 inches (112 cm) long. Cut the 44-inch (112 cm) length into 2 pieces measuring approximately 7 × 44 inches (18 × 112 cm). Sew end to end, making one piece that measures approximately 7 × 88 inches (18 × 224 cm). Remove selvages. Place the 7-inch (18 cm) wide length between the two wider ones and sew together, making a backing that measures approximately 86 × 86 inches (220 × 220 cm).

Binding:

Cut 8 strips measuring 2½ inches (6.5 cm) wide from selvage to selvage. Remove selvages. Sew end to end.

ASSEMBLING

Assembling the blocks:

Alternate dark and light colors. For half the blocks, start the even rounds with light colors and start the odd rounds with dark colors. Starting in the center, sew the shorter Round 1 logs to the center, then sew the longer Round 1 logs to the center. Continue in the manner until 4 rounds are completed.

Alternate dark even round blocks with odd round blocks and sew 7 blocks for each row. Make 7 rows.

Sew rows together.

Border:

Sew the shorter border lengths to the sides. Sew the longer border lengths to the top and bottom.

FINISHING

Press. Layer top, batting, and backing. Baste. With white thread, quilt wavy lines inside some of the logs in each block. Meander on the border.
Trim. Bind.

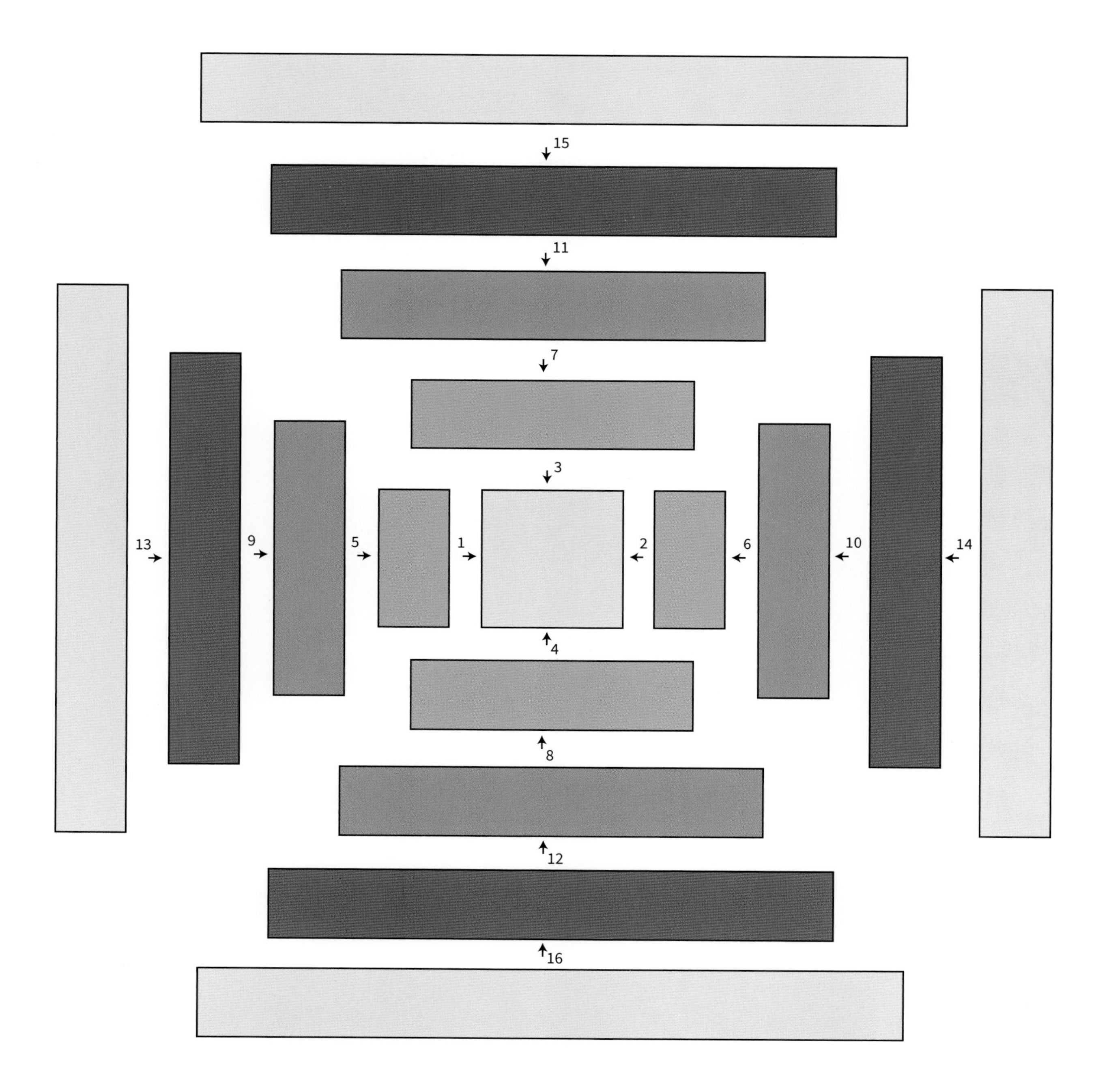

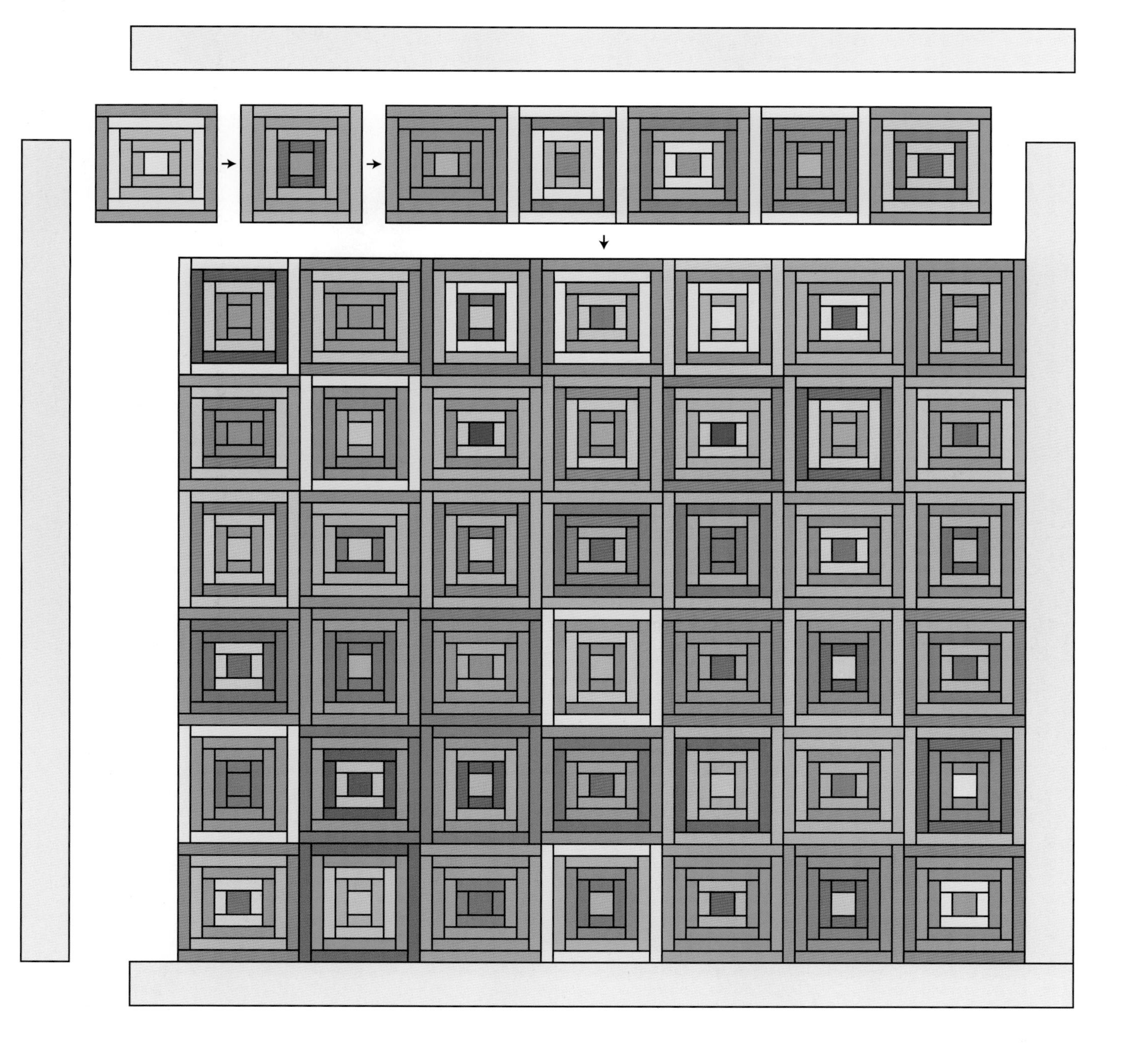

BLOOMERS

The trick here is to pick clear, graphic flowers, large and small, that have clarity of form in this great colorful mixing bowl of a quilt. If the prints don't have enough contrast, or if they are too tonal, they will mush together, and you lose the articulateness that I think is important here. Choose sharply defined subjects of your choosing, from large-scale to medium in size. The color balance is key. All darks or lights or high contrast. If multicolored, like mine, have two or three predominant colors to simplify and hold the madness together.

FINISHED SIZE

75 × 69 inches
(190.5 × 175 cm)
This quilt is quite easy to make. There are 4 sizes of squares, and they nest together without needing to do partial seams or set in seams.

FABRIC CHOICES

It is not possible to offer a specific amount for each fabric. For the small squares, scraps may be sufficient. For the large squares, half yards (46 cm) or bigger will be the best sizes to collect. The goal is to have enough large-scale florals in amounts that will allow fussy cutting, so that the blossoms are featured in the center of most squares.

Backing:
4¾ yards (4.3 m)

Binding:
¾ yard (68.5 cm)

CUTTING

The large squares are cut 12½ × 12½ inches (32 × 32 cm). Cut 8 squares.
The medium-large squares are 9½ × 9½ inches (24 × 24 cm). Cut 15 squares.
The small-medium squares are cut 6½ × 6½ inches (16.5 × 16.5 cm).
Cut 54 squares.
The small squares are cut 3½ × 3½ inches (9 × 9 cm). Cut 96 squares.

ASSEMBLING

It is important to use a design wall to arrange the squares in order to move the pieces around to get a good color mix. Notice that the squares are sewn in units in a sequence that make it possible to do easy piecing. Follow the diagram to sew together.

Backing:

Cut into 2 lengths measuring approximately 40 × 84 inches (102 × 210 cm). Remove selvages. Sew together to make a backing that measures approximately 80 × 84 inches (200 × 210 cm).

Binding:

Cut eight 2½-inch (6.5 cm) wide strips from selvage to selvage. Remove selvages. Sew end to end.

FINISHING

Press. Layer top, batting, and backing. Baste. Quilt around each blossom.
Trim. Bind.

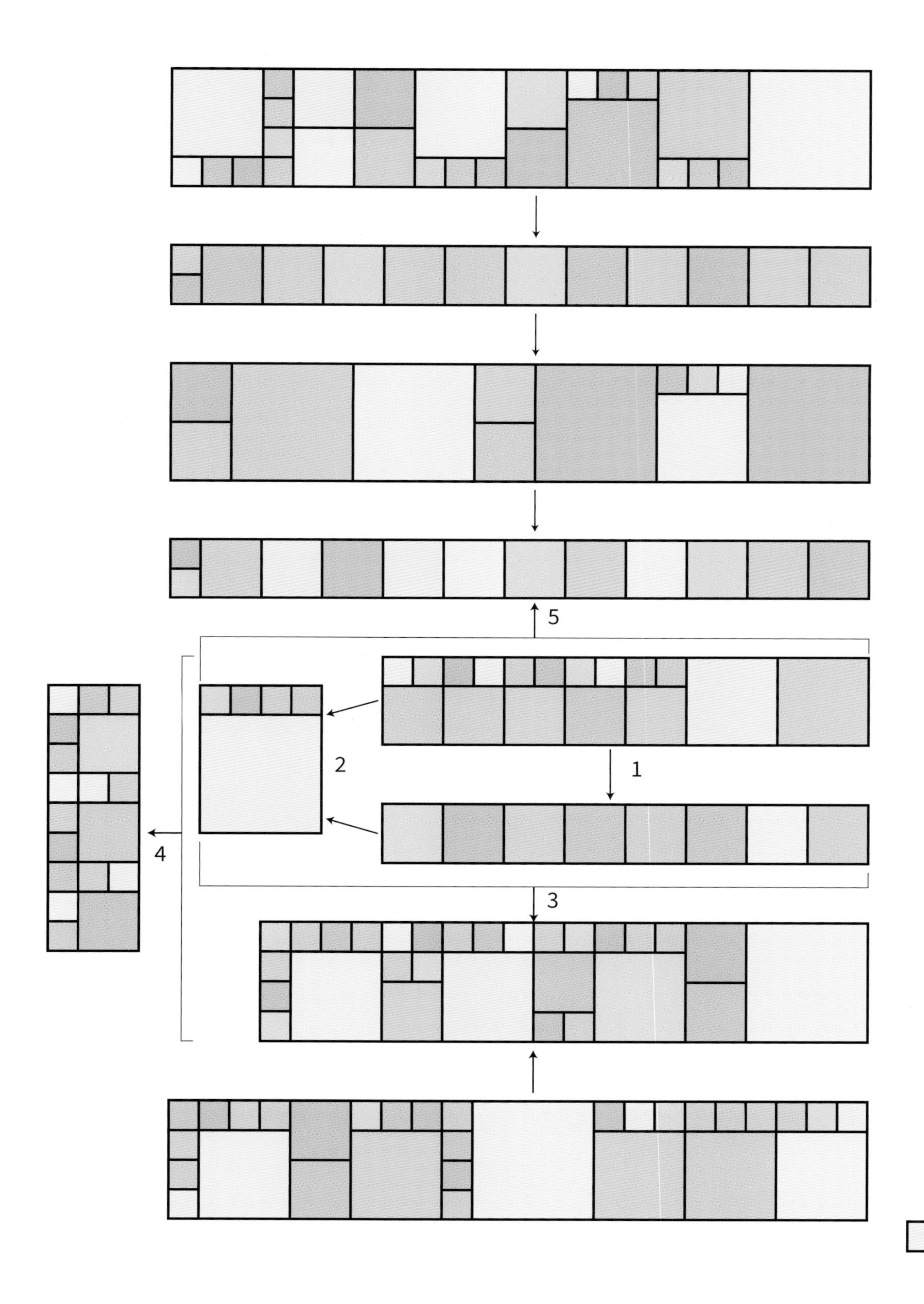
5
2
1
4
3
= 3″

FLOWERS IN THE MIST

Pick a palette that is quite close in tone, be it dark or light. Then pick flowers (or any subject) that almost gets lost in the base of each block and sash with a close, but just definable, print. A good large-scale border in the same mood is a grand finish.

FINISHED SIZE

66 × 79 inches
(167.5 × 200.5 cm)

FABRIC CHOICES

Many of these fabrics from the Kaffe Fassett Collective are currently in print. Adding other fabrics from your stash can make it uniquely yours.

- 2 yards (183 cm) Japanese Chrysanthemum Blush
- 2 yards (183 cm) Brassica White
- 1½ yards (137 cm) Flower Net Black
- ¼ to ½ yard (23 to 46 cm) each Shaggy Neutral, Dorothy Contrast, Charlotte Contrast, Charlotte Pastel, Van Gogh Blue, Japanese Chrysanthemum Contrast, and Amaryllis Lavender

Backing:
5 yards (4.6 m)

Binding:
¾ yard Spot Bottle

CUTTING

The flowers are fussy cut. Find your favorite blossoms and cut squares measuring 6½ × 6½ inches (16.5 × 16.5 cm). Cut a total of 20 fussy-cut blossom squares.
Use Brassica White for the frames around the blossoms. Cut four 11½ inch (29 cm) wide strips from selvage to selvage. Then crosscut 3 strips at 3 inches (7.5 cm), making thirteen 3 × 11½-inch (7.5 × 29 cm) rectangles from each. Cut a total of 39 rectangles. From the last 11½-inch (7.5 cm) strip, crosscut one 3 × 11½-inch (7.5 × 29 cm) rectangle and one 3 × 6½-inch (7.5 × 16.5 cm) rectangle.
Cut three 6½-inch (16.5 cm) wide strips from selvage to selvage. Then crosscut to make thirteen 3 × 6½-inch (7.5 × 16.5 cm) rectangles from each, making 39 rectangles. These 39 are added to the 1 cut previously, making a total of 40 rectangles.
The sashing is semi-fussy cut. Cut strips of Flower Net Black so that the flowers are featured in or near the center of the strip. Cut 17 strips 2½ inches (6.5 cm) wide from selvage to selvage. Remove the selvages and sew end to end.
Then cut 6 lengths measuring 54½ inches (138.5 cm) for the horizontal sashing.
Cut 25 lengths measuring 11½ inches (29 cm) for the vertical sashings.
Cut Japanese Chrysanthemum Blush into 2 lengths measuring 6½ × 67½ inches (16.5 × 171.5 cm). Cut 2 lengths measuring 6½ × 66½ inches (16.5 × 169 cm).

Backing:

Cut 2 lengths measuring approximately 87 inches (221 cm) long. Remove selvages and sew together, making a backing that measures approximately 80 × 87 inches (200 × 230 cm). Trim to approximately 74 × 87 inches (188 × 230 cm).

Binding:

Cut eight 2½ inch (6.5 cm) wide strips from selvage to selvage. Remove selvage. Sew end to end.

ASSEMBLING

For each block, choose one blossom square, two 6½-inch (16.5 cm) Brassica rectangles, and two 11½-inch (29 cm) Brassica rectangles. Sew together as shown in the diagram. Make 20 blocks.
Alternate 5 vertical sashing strips and 4 blocks and sew to make rows. Make 5 rows. Alternate 6 horizontal sashing strips with the block rows. Sew together.
Sew the longer borders to the sides. Sew the remaining borders to the top and bottom.

FINISHING

Press. Layer top, batting, and backing. Baste. Using a gray thread, quilt around the blossoms and meander throughout the rest.
Trim. Bind.

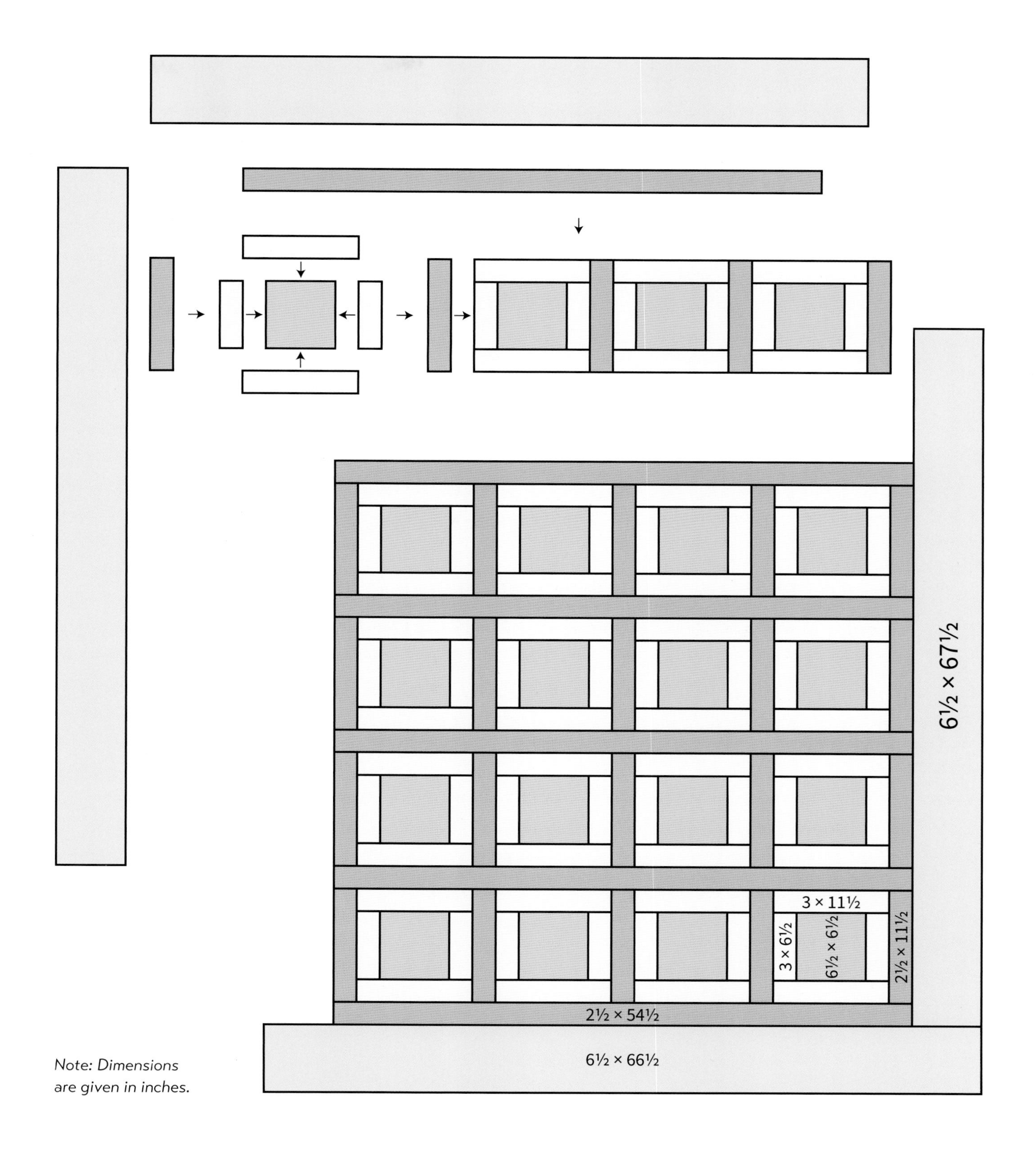

Note: Dimensions are given in inches.

FLORAL CHECKERBOARD

Anybody who has followed my output over the years will know that the Snowball block is one I return to often. I love the simple placement of squares with the corners cut off to create the illusion of a circle.

It is a great form to show off the big-scale florals of the Kaffe Fassett Collective fabrics. Large Peonies, Dahlias, and Cactus Flowers join Chrysanthemums, Poppies, and Sunflowers to create this colorful explosion of a quilt. In each nine-patch block, I've used small-scale prints to contrast with the large florals to create a checkerboard effect. I used a neutral shot cotton for the cornerstones of each Snowball, which works for most areas, but if I did it again, I'd use a darker or black fabric for the corners to create a crisper effect. The daisy print on the sashing keeps the floral theme going.

This layout could also be done in many different themes. I can imagine all leaf prints or bold geometrics.

FINISHED SIZE

82 × 82 inches (200 × 200 cm) This is a traditional Snowball pattern arranged in a nine-patch block.

FABRIC CHOICES

All of the fabrics used in this quilt are from the Kaffe Fassett Collective. There are two different scales of prints in the Snowballs. The large-scale florals include Cactus Flower, Van Gogh, Dorothy, Dancing Dahlias, Hokusai's Mums, and Luscious. The smaller-scale fabrics include Ferns, Busy Lizzy, and Moss Flower. The sashing is Lucy, and the cornerstones are Guinea Flower. Shot Cotton is used in the corners of the Snowballs. There are a total of 144 Snowballs.

½ to ¾ yard (46 to 68.5 cm) each of fifteen different large-scale florals. The amount will depend on choosing five large blossoms of each print to make 6½-inch (16.5 cm) squares.

½ yard (46 cm) each of 10 to 12 small- to medium-scale florals

2¼ yards (2 m) Shot Cotton Shadow or any dark-colored Shot Cotton or solid fabric

1½ yards (1.37 m) Lucy Lavender or a medium-scale monochromatic print floral for sashing strips

½ yard (46 cm) Guinea Flower Purple for cornerstones

Backing:

6½ yards (6 m)

Binding:

¾ yard (68.5 cm) Guinea Flower Purple

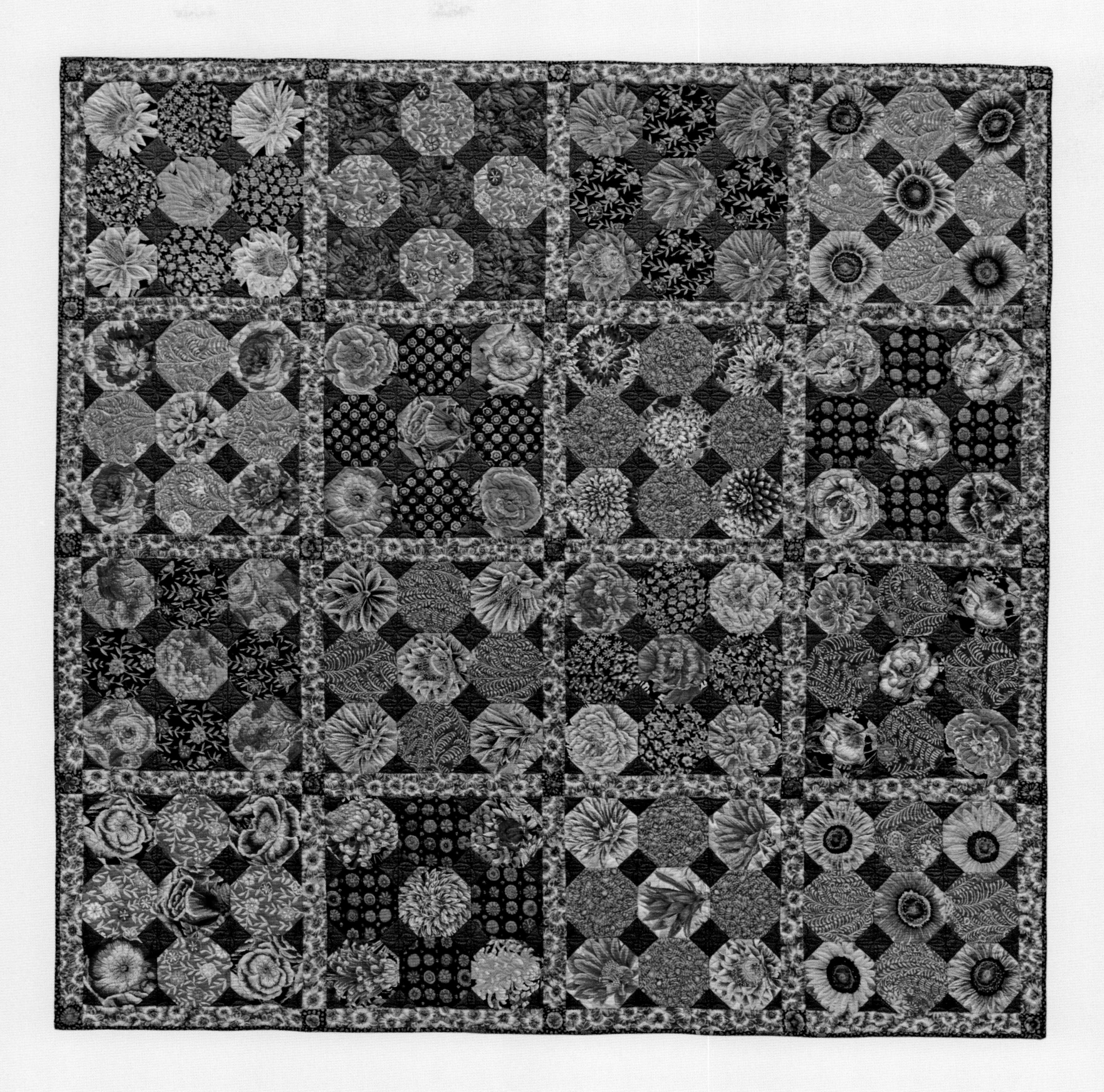

CUTTING

Each block has 5 fussy cut blossoms measuring 6½ × 6½ inches (16.5 × 16.5 cm) and 4 small prints cut to 6½ × 6½ inches (16.5 × 16.5 cm). Cut sets of fussy blossom squares and small print squares to make 16 blocks with 9 Snowballs each.

Shot Cotton:

Cut thirty-four 2¼ inch (6 cm) wide strips from selvage to selvage. Crosscut at 2¼ inches (6 cm), making 17 squares from each strip.

Sashing:

Cut 2 strips measuring 18½ inches (47 cm) wide from selvage to selvage. Crosscut at 2½ inches (6.5 cm). Each strip will yield 16 rectangles. Cut 4 strips 2½ inches (6.5 cm) wide from selvage to selvage and crosscut at 18½ inches (47 cm), making 2 rectangles from each. There should be a total of 40 rectangles.

Cornerstones:

Fussy cut blossoms from Guinea Flower or any small floral print. Cut 25 squares measuring 2½ × 2½ inches (6.5 × 6.5 cm).

Backing:

Cut 2 lengths measuring approximately 90 inches (230 cm) long. Cut one length approximately 46 inches (117 cm) long.
Cut the 46-inch (117 cm) length into 2 pieces measuring approximately 11 × 46 inches (28 × 117 cm). Sew end to end, making that piece approximately 11 × 90 inches (28 × 230 cm). Remove selvages. Place the 11 inch (28 cm) wide length between the wider ones and sew together, making a backing that measures approximately 90 × 90 inches (230 × 230 cm).

Binding:

Cut 9 strips measuring 2½ inches (6.5 cm) from selvage to selvage. Remove selvages. Sew end to end.

ASSEMBLING

Making the Snowball blocks:
For each block, choose 5 matching blossom squares, 4 matching smaller-scale squares, and 36 Shot Cotton squares.
Follow the diagram to make 9 Snowballs.

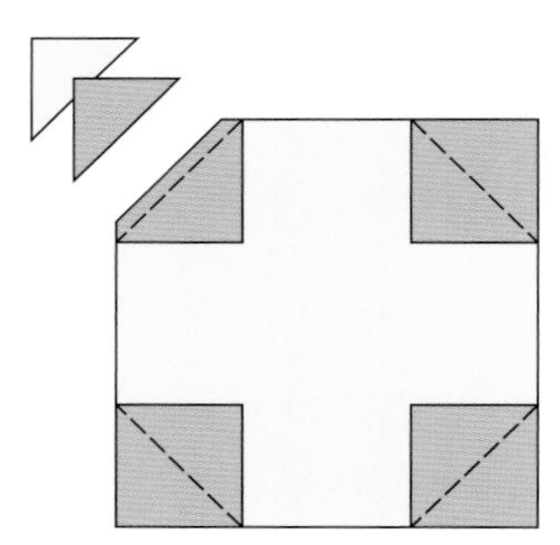

1. Stitch and trim

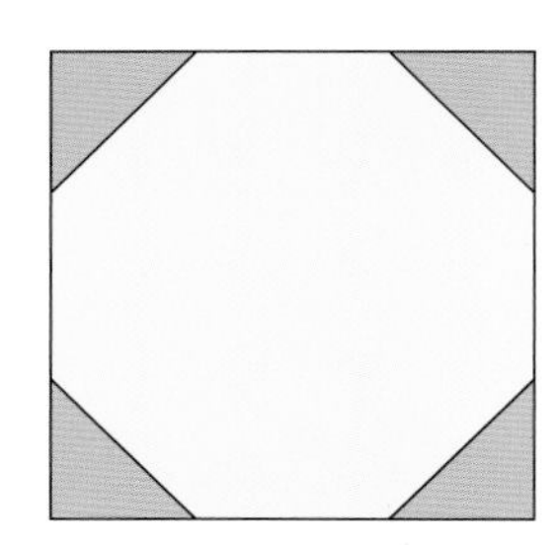

2. Press open

Assembling the 9 patches:

Arrange the 9 Snowballs, alternating the blooms with the small prints.
Sew 3 Snowballs together for each of the 3 rows. Sew rows together.

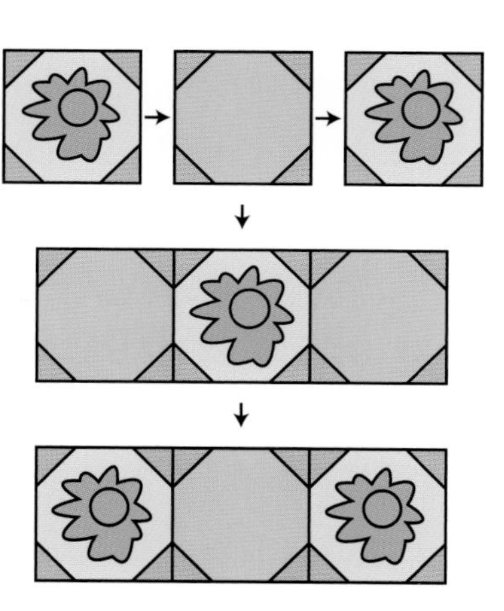

Assembling the top:

Alternate sashing strips with 4 Snowball blocks for each row. Make 4 rows.
Alternate 5 cornerstones with 4 sashing strips to make 5 horizontal sashings.
Alternate 5 horizontal sashing with 4 Snowball rows. Sew together.

FINISHING

Press. Layer top, batting, and backing. Baste. With neutral color thread, meander in the smaller Snowballs and outline the blooms in the bigger Snowballs.
Trim. Bind.

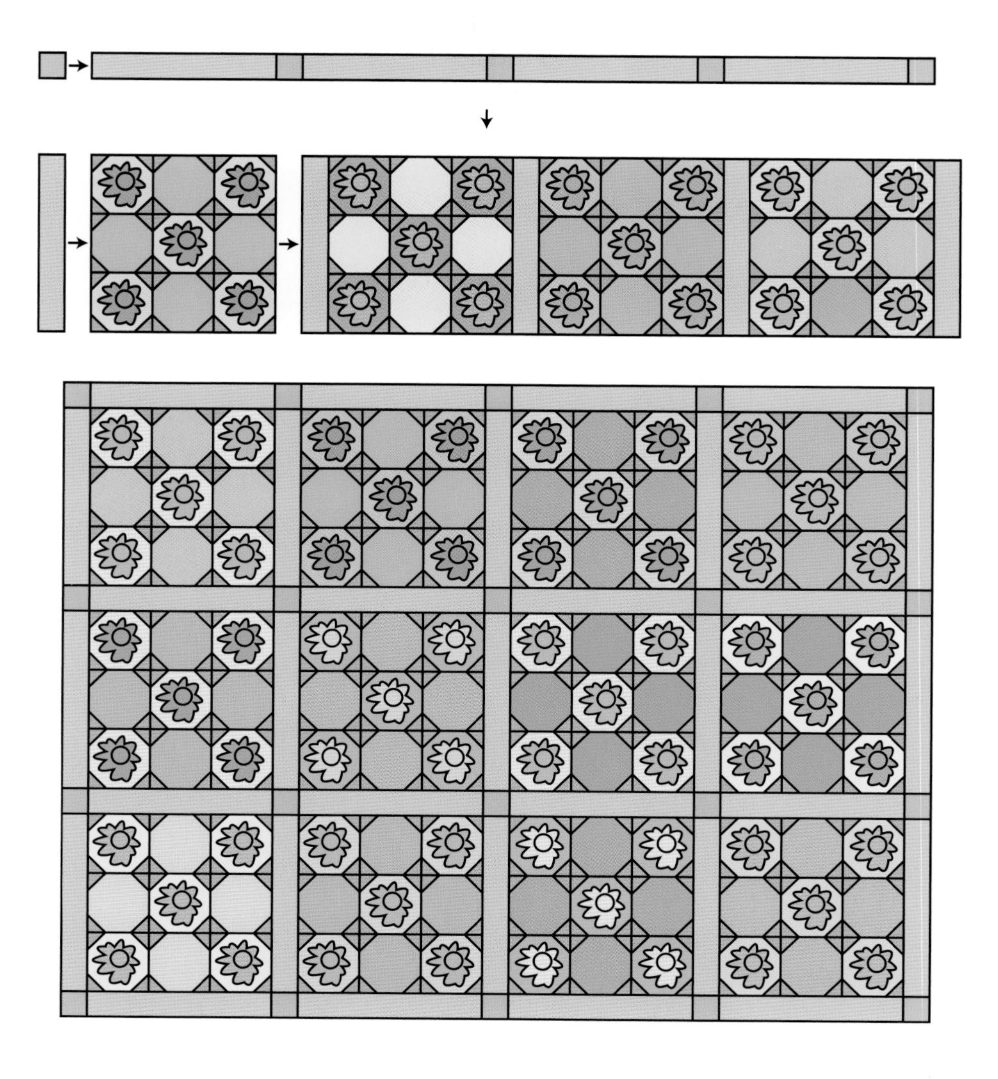

ACKNOWLEDGMENTS

Making this survey of the amazing archive of patterned fabrics we have designed over the past twenty-five years is a task I am glad to share with the woman who brought me into this glorious world of patchwork, Liza Lucy. We have coordinated on quilts, books, and, best of all, the extraordinary flow of prints that have found a worldwide audience. So, deepest gratitude to Liza for making quilts and constantly advising on our book- and print-related decisions, and to her team of makers, Bobbi Penniman, Mira Mayer, and Bundle Backhouse, as well as to Judy Irish for the quilting of most of our quilts.

When I say "our," I mean myself and Brandon Mably, who is the constant in my life, who plans all the photo shoots and the making of quilts and is an important designer on the Kaffe Fassett Collective, our two annual collections of prints. He also took many of the inspiration shots in this book. Thanks also to Philip Jacobs in his consistent flow of handsome designs.

As always, hugest thanks to our talented photographer, Debbie Patterson, who has so faithfully added her magic eye to our annual books, but especially to this and our other hardback books. Thanks to editors Meredith Clark and Teresa Duryea Wong as well as Shawna Mullen for taking up the reins. Thanks to Bundle Backhouse, who coordinates all our travels, exhibitions, and photo shoots, as well as checking patterns and keeping a watchful eye over the endless details on a book like this.

I very much want to acknowledge our gorgeous locations. Thanks to Rupert Spira for creating the stunning tile panels that gave our quilts such rich backgrounds, and much gratitude to all the people of that quirky little street in East London, Aberfeldy Street, who painted the perfect selections of colorful backgrounds for most of our quilts. Thanks also to the Victorian engineers who produced Smithfield Market and many of London's bridges.

Thanks to Bernina, Aurifil, Paper Pieces, and the FreeSpirit Fabrics team for their unstinting support. Last, huge appreciation to Liz Dougherty at FreeSpirit Fabrics for arranging our workshop tours, and to all the fabric shops that host us and the inspiring consumers who motivate us designers with their surprising use of our prints.

Thank you also to Hugh Ehrman for his continuing support. Many of the tapestries shown in the book are available as kits from Ehrman Tapestry.

Thanks to the following people for permitting me to use their photographs:

Recep Imal for his photo of colorful agate, page 77.

Teresa Duryea Wong for the use of her photo of Fushimi Inari Shrine in Kyoto, page 8.

Ehrman Tapestry for the use of the photo of the Glorious Bouquet flower panel, page 105.

(Debbie Patterson created the principal photography, and Brandon Mably and I added inspiration images, from our archives, throughout.)

Thanks to tech editors Emilija K. Mayer Gross, Mira Mayer, and Betsey Westover.

Lastly, I want to acknowledge Abrams's brilliant art department, who always thrill us with their exciting, fresh layouts of our material.

Editor: Meredith A. Clark
Designer: Jenice Kim
Managing Editor: Lisa Silverman
Production Manager: Kathleen Gaffney

Library of Congress Control Number: 2022942352

ISBN: 978-1-4197-6140-9
eISBN: 978-1-64700-649-5

Printed and bound in China
10 9 8 7 6 5 4 3 2 1

ABRAMS The Art of Books
195 Broadway, New York, NY 10007
abramsbooks.com